MATRIMONIAL INDISSOLUBILITY: CONTRARY CONDITIONS

i

This dissertation was approved by the Very Reverend
John Rogg Schmidt, A.B., LL.B., J.C.D., as Director,
and by the Right Reverend Thomas Owen Martin,
Ph.D., S.T.D., J.C.D., LL.M., and the Reverend
Romaeus W. O'Brien, O. Carm., J.C.D., as Readers.

The Catholic University of America
Canon Law Studies
No. 377

MATRIMONIAL INDISSOLUBILITY: CONTRARY CONDITIONS

A Historical Synopsis and a Commentary

A DISSERTATION

*Submitted to the Faculty of the School of Canon Law
of the Catholic University of America in Partial
Fulfillment of the Requirements for the
Degree of Doctor of Canon Law*

BY THE

REV. DENNIS J. BURNS, A.B., J.C.L.
Priest of the Archdiocese of Boston

THE CATHOLIC UNIVERSITY OF AMERICA PRESS
Washington, D.C.

1963

Nihil Obstat: Ioannes Rogg Schmidt, J.C.D.
Censor Deputatus
Washingtonii, die 14, maii, 1957

Imprimatur: Richardus Iacobus Cushing, D.D.
Archiepiscopus Bostoniensis
Bostonii, die 19. maii, 1957

Printed by
SULLIVAN BROS., PRINTERS
Lowell, Massachusetts

Respectfully Dedicated

with

Reverence and Gratitude

to

His Eminence

Richard Cardinal Cushing, D.D.

Archbishop of Boston

and to

My Mother and Father

FOREWORD

From the beginning the Creator made man and woman and united them in a union of body and spirit. This union was the contract of marriage. In the course of human history, because of the weakness and malice of men, the primitive nature of this contract, one, sacred and indissoluble, was perverted from that state as instituted by the Author of Nature. Christ, the Son of God, the Restorer of all things, restored this institution also to its primal dignity and perpetual stability and, for the baptized, elevated the natural contract of marriage to the status of a sacrament. This is the teaching of the Sacred Scriptures, the constant tradition of the Universal Church, the solemn definition of the Council of Trent, the law of the Code of Canon Law.

Although this institution of matrimony is thus of divine origin, it cannot be effected without the co-operation of the human will. Marriage can arise only from the consent of the contracting parties, by which each gives and accepts the conjugal rights and obligations of the married state. This consent is so necessary that no human power can supply it, if the parties thereto do not. The primary end of marriage is the procreation and education of children; its essential properties are unity and indissolubility. Together, these elements, the primary end and the essential properties, constitute the substance of the marriage, so that the human consent to the contract must extend to these, or there is no true marriage.

This matrimonial consent may be given by the parties in an absolute manner, or it may be made dependent on the fulfillment of some condition. If the conditional consent is such that it is made dependent on the fulfillment of a condition which is against some substantial element of marriage, that condition will invalidate the matrimonial contract thus entered. If, therefore, one or both of the parties make the consent to that marriage contract dependent on a condition which is contrary to the essential perpetuity of the bond, that contract is invalid; no marriage is effected.

The present study will attempt to present the historical development of the teaching of the Church on the matter of the invalidating effect of such a condition which, when incorporated in the consent, is contrary to the perpetuity of the marriage bond. It aims, in addition, to present a canonical commentary on the legislation of the Code of Canon Law in reference to such conditions. This work thus falls into a natural division of two sections. The first, a historical synopsis, will trace the development of doctrine from the theological expression of the matter in Saint Augustine, through the wealth of canonical writings, to the legislation of the Code of Canon Law. The second section, a commentary on this legislation, will endeavor to indicate the nature of such conditions against the substance of marriage and, specifically, against the indissolubility of the bond. This calls not only for a consideration of the theory and teaching of the canonists, but also for a study of the jurisprudence of the ecclesiastical courts and of the doctrinal clarification afforded by the application of juridical doctrine to the solution of practical cases presented for judgment.

In the present work, the scope of the commentary is limited to the legislation of the Church and its prudent application in the adjudication of cases involving such conditions contrary to the essential stability of marriage. The condition of this sort is differentiated from similar additions or modifications of the contract, and from a speculative error about the nature of marriage, which may or may not cause such a condition to be added. The difference of requirements for the existence of invalidity in reality and for the *external proof* of such invalidity in the eyes of the ecclesiastical tribunals will be noted.

One must note it as evident, however, in discussing the field of intellect and will, and in studying the juridical effects of the interplay between them, that there will remain a vast difference between the establishment of principles and the application of these principles to individual cases in the external forum of the Church. Much of the work of the ecclesiastical tribunal must deal with an analysis of the internal dispositions of mind and will of the parties to the contract. For this reason, the applications of law may not always mirror the actual, objective status of the marriage involved. In judging marriage cases, therefore, the tribunals of the Church do not declare that a marriage is definitely valid: *constat de validitate,* but rather declare that the invalidity of the marriage has not been conclusively proved: *non constat de nullitate*. This is the natural consequence of the necessity for social order, namely that the invalidity of an apparent marriage be proved conclusively before that union will be declared null. A deeper investigation of the thought and will processes must remain the task of philosophers and psychologists.

The author wishes to express his sincere and heartfelt thanks to His Eminence, the Most Reverend Richard Cardinal Cushing, D.D., Archbishop of Boston, for the opportunity of pursuing higher studies, to the members of the Faculty of the School of Canon Law, especially the Reverend Director and Readers of this dissertation, for their generous guidance and assistance, and to all others who have contributed to this work.

"By matrimony, therefore, the souls of the contracting parties are joined and knit together more directly and more intimately than are their bodies, and that not by any passing affection of sense or spirit, but by a deliberate and firm act of the will, and from this union of souls, by God's decree, a sacred and inviolable bond arises."

Pope Pius XI, *Casti connubii*

TABLE OF CONTENTS

PART I
HISTORICAL SYNOPSIS

CHAPTER I

THE ORIGIN AND DEVELOPMENT OF THE DOCTRINE ON INDISSOLUBILITY

ARTICLE I. DIVINE REVELATION

If we seek the origin of the indissolubility of the marriage bond, we find it in the earliest days of man's existence, when God created woman and united her to the first man in the marriage contract. The indissolubility of that contract was indicated in the words of Adam, divinely inspired: "This now is bone of my bones and flesh of my flesh; she shall be called woman because she was taken out of man. Wherefore a man shall leave father and mother and shall cleave to his wife and they shall be two in one flesh,"[1] so that the marriage union makes them as one. When, in the New Testament, Christ spoke of this contract of marriage, He taught clearly and definitely the doctrine of its indissoluble character. In His Sermon on the Mount, He spoke forcefully against the continuance of the concession of the Old Dispensation: "It was said, moreover: 'Whoever puts away his wife, let him give her a written notice of dismissal.' But I say to you that everyone who puts away his wife, save on account of immorality, causes her to commit adultery; and he who marries a woman who has been put away commits adultery."[2]

Christ also declared the authentic interpretation of the words of Adam above, attributing them to divine inspiration: "There came to Him some Pharisees, testing Him, and saying 'Is it lawful for a man to put his wife away for any cause?' But He answered and said to them, 'Have you not read that the Creator, from the beginning, made them male and female, and said, 'For this cause a man shall leave his father and mother, and cleave to his wife, and the two shall become one flesh?' Therefore now they are no longer two, but one flesh. What therefore God has joined together, let no man put asunder."[3]

---

[1] Genesis, II: 23-24, The Holy Bible translated from the Latin Vulgate (Douay-Rheims version, C. Wildermann Co., Inc., New York, 1912).

[2] Matthew, V: 31-32, Cf. also Mark, X: 11, and Luke, XVI: 18, The New Testament (Confraternity Edition, St. Anthony Guild Press, Paterson, N. J., 1944).

[3] Matthew, XIX: 3-8. Cf. also Mark, X: 2-9.

This teaching of Christ was clearly understood by His followers. St. Paul, writing to the Corinthians, stated: "But to those who are married, not I, but the Lord commands that a wife is not to depart from her husband, and if she departs, that she is to remain unmarried or be reconciled to her husband. And let not a husband put away his wife."[4] Paul gave the reason for this in a letter to his Roman converts: "The married woman is bound by the Law while her husband is alive; but if her husband die, she is set free from the law of her husband. Therefore, while her husband is alive, she will be called an adulteress if she be with another man."[5]

These texts clearly indicate that the doctrine of the indissolubility of the marriage contract is to be found initially in the clear teachings of the Holy Scriptures, inspired of God.[6]

Article II. The Theology of St. Augustine

The development of this doctrine on the indissolubility of marriage as an early target for error was theological rather than properly canonical. The doctrine of St. Augustine (354-430) was, however, the constant source of reference for the canonical writers of later ages, and it seems useful to present it here for consultation when necessary in studying the writings of later canonical commentators.

In four of his works St. Augustine explained this doctrine and expanded it with his logical conclusions. His words were repeated,

---

[4] I Corinthians, VII: 10-11.

[5] Romans, VII: 1-3.

[6] "Quidquid autem est de iure mere naturali sive primario sive secundario, iam certum est vinculum matrimoniale, etiam praecisione facta ab elevatione contractus matrimonialis ad naturam sacramenti, sive in Ecclesia sive extra Ecclesiam ab ipso initio creationis, esse omnino insolubile saltem ex iure positivo divino, quod facile probari potest ex divina revelatione." — Coronata, *Institutiones Iuris Canonici, De Sacramentis Tractatus Canonicus*, Vol. III, *De Matrimonio et de Sacramentalibus* (Romae: Marietti, 1943), n. 10, p. 13 (hereafter cited *De Matrimonio*). Cf. also Sipos, *Enchiridion Iuris Canonici* (6 ed. a L. Gálas, Romae: Herder, 1954), § 97, p. 407; Vlaming, *Praelectiones Iuris Matrimonii* (4, ed. a L. Bender, Bussum in Hollandia: Paulus Brand, 1950), Art. II, p. 16 (hereafter cited *Praelectiones*); Bayon, *Tractatus Canonico-Moralis de Sacramento Matrimonii* (2 vols. in 1, Madrid, 1931), n. 44, p. 19 (hereafter cited *De Sacramento Matrimonii*);Wernz-Vidal, *Ius Matrimoniale* (3. ed. a P. Aguirre, Romae: Apud Aedes Universitatis Gregorianae, 1946), n. 622, pp. 784-785; De Becker, *De Sponsalibus et Matrimonio Praelectiones Canonicae* (editio nova, Louvain: Fr. Ceuterick, 1931), Sect. IX, pp. 414-415 (hereafter cited *De Sponsalibus et Matrimonio*).

verbatim in many cases, in the sources of Canon Law as the foundation of modern law. Much of the technical terminology, now universally used, had its origin in his writings.

St. Augustine indicated a threefold benefit of marriage, the three blessings of the contract, as the *"bonum prolis"*, the blessing of offspring, the *"bonum fidei"*, the blessing of fidelity, and *"bonum sacramenti"*, the blessing of indissolubility. Citing the words of the Apostle, he wrote:

"Bonum ergo nuptiae in omnibus quae sunt propria nuptiarum. Haec autem sunt tria, generandi ordinatio, fides pudicitiae, connubii sacramentum. Propter ordinationem generandi scriptum est: 'Volo iuniores nubere, filios procreare, matrifamilias esse'. Propter fidem pudicitiae: 'Uxor non habet potestatem sui corporis, sed vir; similiter et vir non habet potestatem sui corporis, sed mulier'. Propter connubii sacramentum: 'Quod Deus conjunxit, homo non separet'." [7]

He refuted the error of those who insisted that marriage is essentially evil, asserting rather:

"Id quod bonum habent nuptiae et quo bonae sunt nuptiae, peccatum esse nunquam potest. Hoc autem tripertitum est: fides, proles, sacramentum. In fide attenditur ne praeter vinculum conjugale cum altera vel altero concumbatur; in prole, ut amanter suscipiatur, benigne nutriatur, religiose educetur; in sacramento, ut conjugium non separetur et dimissus aut dimissa nec causa prolis alteri conjungatur." [8]

Regarding the third blessing of indissolubility, St. Augustine declared it is an essential property of the contract of Christian marriage:

"Bonum igitur nuptiarum per omnes gentes atque omnes homines in causa generandi est et in fide castitatis; quod autem ad populum Dei pertinet, etiam in sanctitate sacramenti, per quam nefas est etiam repudio discedentem alteri nubere, dum

---

[7] *De Peccato Originali contra Pelagium*, Liber II, Cap. 34—Migne, *Patrologiae Cursus Completus, Series Latina* (221 vols., Parisiis, 1844-1864) XXXXIV, 404 (hereafter cited as MPL).

[8] *De Genesi ad Litteram*, Liber IX, Cap. 7—*Corpus Scriptorum Ecclesiasticorum Latinorum* (74 vols. incomplete, Vindobonae, 1866—) XXVIII, Sect. III, Pars 1, 275-6 (hereafter cited *CSEL*).

vir eius vivit, nec saltem ipsa causa pariendi; quae cum sola sit qua nuptiae fiunt, nec ea re non subsequente propter quam fiunt solvitur vinculum nuptiale nisi conjugis morte." [9]
This indissolubility of the bond, according to Augustine, persists regardless of whether or not the husband and wife remain together.

"Siquidem interveniente divortio non aboletur illa confoederatio nuptialis, ita ut sibi conjuges sint etiam separati, cum illis autem adulterium committant, quibus fuerint etiam post suum repudium copulati, vel illa viro vel ille mulieri. Nec tamen nisi in civitate Dei nostri, in monte sancto eius talis est causa cum uxore." [10]
In one of his sermons to the married, he declared in the same vein:

"Non vobis licet habere uxores, quarum priores mariti vivunt; nec vobis, feminae, habere viros licet, quorum priores uxores vivunt. Adulterina sunt ista conjugia non jure fori, sed jure coeli. Nec eam feminam quae per repudium discessit a marito licet vobis ducere, vivo marito. Solius fornicationis causa licet uxorem adulteram dimittere; sed illa vivente non licet alteram ducere. Et vobis, feminae, nec illos viros a quibus per repudium discesserunt uxores eorum, maritos habere conceditur; non licet: adulteria sunt, non conjugia." [11]
This perpetual bond of marriage bound the married couple who had separated from each other more intimately than the physical bond of an adulterous union.

"Usque adeo manent inter viventes semel inita jura nuptiarum, ut potius sint inter se conjuges qui ab alterutro separati sint quam cum his quibus aliis adhaeserunt. Cum aliis quippe adulteri non essent, nisi ad alterutrum conjuges permanerent. Ita manet inter viventes quiddam conjugale, quod nec separatio nec cum altero copulatio possit auferre." [12]
Even a sinful union of concubinage could become a valid marriage by the subsequent giving of full consent to a permanent union.

[9] *De Bono Conjugali*, Cap. XXIV—*CSEL*, XXXXI, 226-7.
[10] *De Bono Conjugali*, Cap. VII—*CSEL*, XXXXI, 197.
[11] *Sermo CCCXCII*, *(Ad Conjugatos)*, Cap. II — *MPL*, XXXIX (1865), col. 1710.
[12] *De Nuptiis et Concupiscentia*, Lib. I, Cap. 10—*CSEL*, XXXXII, 223.

"Ita nec concubinae ad tempus adhibitae, si filiorum causa concumbant, justum faciunt concubinatum suum; nec conjugatae, si cum maritis lasciviant, nuptiali ordini crimen imponunt. Posse sane fieri nuptias ex male conjunctis honesto postea placito consequente manifestum est." [13]

A valid marriage among Christians, however, once entered into and consummated, bound both parties until the death of one of them.

"Semel autem initum connubium in civitate Dei nostri, ubi etiam ex prima duorum hominum copula quoddam sacramentum nuptiae gerunt, nullo modo potest nisi alicuius eorum morte dissolvi." [14]

In his work *De Bono Conjugali,* St. Augustine furnished a most cogent explanation of the essential properties of the marriage contract. He did this in a passage which, known as the *Solet Quaeri,* was to be cited repeatedly in the *Corpus Iuris Canonici* as the basic document for this doctrine. The *Solet Quaeri* declared that the essential character of the blessing of the sacrament rested in the necessary intention of indissolubility for the marriage union, if that union was truly to be considered a marriage.

"Solet etiam quaeri, cum masculus et femina, nec ille maritus, nec illa uxor alterius, sibimet non filiorum procreandorum, sed propter incontinentiam solius concubitus causa copulantur, ea fide media, ut nec ille cum altera, nec illa cum altero id faciat, utrum nuptiae sint vocandae, et potest quidem fortasse non absurde hoc appellari connubium, si usque ad mortem alicuius eorum id inter eos placuerit, et prolis generationem, quamvis non ea causa conjuncti sint, non tamen vitaverint, ut vel nolint sibi nasci filios vel etiam opere aliquo malo agant, ne nascantur, ceterum si vel utrumque vel unum horum desit, non invenio quemadmodum has nuptias appellare possimus; etiam si aliquam sibi vir ad tempus adhibuerit, donec aliam dignam vel honoribus vel facultatibus suis inveniat, quam comparem

---

[13] *De Bono Conjugali,* Cap. XIV—*CSEL* XXXXI, 209. Manifestly the quotation does not deal with a liaison with an already married man; for otherwise this text would have been at complete variance with the evident mind of St. Augustine.

[14] *Ibid.,* Cap. XV—*CSEL, loc. cit.*

ducat, ipso animo adulter est, nec cum illa, quam cupit invenire, sed cum ista, cum qua sic cubat, ut cum ea non habeat maritale consortium, unde et ipsa hoc sciens ac volens impudice utique miscetur ei, cum quo non habet foedus uxorium." [15] Accordingly, St. Augustine appeared ready to dignify even an otherwise irregular union with the name of marriage, if the substantial elements of unity and indissolubility were retained, together with the primary end of marriage.

In applying this doctrine to the marriage of Our Lady and St. Joseph, St. Augustine declared that theirs was a true marriage contract, when studied in the light of these essential elements of the threefold blessing of marriage:

"Omne igitur nuptiarum bonum impletum est in illis parentibus Christi: proles, fides, sacramentum. Prolem cognoscamus ipsum dominum Jesum; fidem, quia nullum adulterium, sacramentum, quia nullum divortium." [16]

There are many other texts which might be cited,[17] but the texts already reproduced sufficiently indicate how the doctrine of Christ, clarified by St. Paul, was developed theologically by St. Augustine. One reads nothing about attached conditions whose effect could be that of vitiating the marriage contract. This is not surprising, since the contractual aspect of marriage had not been worked out thoroughly as yet.[18]

Article III. Early Canonical Development

A. Anselm of Lucca—Collectio Canonum

Towards the end of the eleventh century a more distinct line was being drawn between doctrinal theology and canon law. In the work of Anselm of Lucca (c. 1083) one finds matters treated from the specific viewpoint of canonical legislation. The teaching of St.

---

[15] *De Bono Conjugali*, Cap. V—*CSEL*, XXXXI, 193-4.
[16] *De Nuptiis et Concupiscentia*, Liber I, Cap. 11—*CSEL*, XXXXII, 225.
[17] V. g., cf. *De Nuptiis et Concupiscentia*, Lib. I, Cap. 17—*CSEL*, XXXXII, 231; *De Bono Conjugali*, Cap. III—*CSEL*, XXXXI, 190.
[18] For a detailed, theological discussion of the doctrine of St. Augustine, cf. Amandus Reuter, *S. Aurelii Augustini Doctrina de Bonis Matrimonii*, Analecta Gregoriana, Vol. XXVII (Series Theologica, Sectio B. n. 12), (Romae: Apud Aedes Universitatis Gregorianae, 1942), Pars II, Cap. III, pp. 219-52.

Augustine carried over into the canonical thought and Anselm cited directly much of his doctrine. The *Solet Quaeri* was quoted verbatim,[19] as was the *Nec concubinae ad tempus,* [20] the *Bonum igitur nuptiarum* [21] and the *Non vobis licet.*[22]

B. Ivo of Chartres—Decretum and Panormia

In his work *Decretum* and in the more polished *Panormia,* Ivo of Chartres (d. 1116), like Anselm, his contemporary, quoted verbatim many of the statements of St. Augustine on the nature of the marriage contract.[23]

Because of the profusion of citations which referred to purely doctrinal matter, the *Decretum* of Ivo did not reflect the character of an exclusively canonical work. In this work canonical legislation was commingled with doctrinal texts. Nevertheless, the effect of both the *Decretum* and the *Panormia* on subsequent canonical thought was most important, in consequence of the wide distribution of both works.[24]

C. Decretum of Gratian and the Decretists

The *Decretum* of Gratian (c. 1140) was a systematic textbook which may be regarded as initiating the juridical science of Canon Law. In it the same basic doctrine of Augustine on the essential properties of marriage was incorporated. Gratian quoted the *Solet quaeri* with but a few unimportant verbal changes.[25] The minor changes which occurred in Gratian's quotation of the *Usque adeo* indicated the definite notion of the bond of marriage.[26]

[19] *Anselmi Lucensis Collectio Canonum* (ed. a F. Thaner, Innsbruck, 1906-1915), Liber X, Cap. 10, p. 486.

[20] *Op. cit.,* Lib. X, Cap. 11, p. 487.

[21] *Ibid.,* Cap. XII, p. 487.

[22] *Ibid.,* Cap. XIV, p. 488.

[23] Thus he quoted the *Siquidem, interveniente divortio: Decretum,* Lib. VIII, Cap. 9—*MPL,* CLXI, p. 586; the *Usque adeo: Decretum, op. cit.,* Cap. 12-13—*ibid.,* p. 586; the *Solet quaeri: Decretum,* Cap. 65, *ibid.,* p. 597, and *Panormia,* Lib. VI, Cap. 27—*MPL,* CLXI, pp. 1248-49; the *Omne Itaque: Decretum,* Cap. 15—*ibid.,* p. 587, and *Panormia,* Cap. 30—*ibid.,* p. 1249; the *Nec concubinae ad tempus: Decretum,* Cap. 10—*ibid.,* p. 586, and *Panormia,* Cap. 45—*ibid.,* p. 1253.

[24] Cf. Fournier, *Les Collections Canoniques Attribuées à Yves de Chartres,* (Paris, 1897), Chap. II, pp. 74-76.

[25] C. 6, C. XXXII, q. 2—*Corpus Iuris Canonici* (ed. *Lipsiensis 2., post Aemilii L. Richteri curae instruxit Aemilius Friedberg,* 2 vols., Lipsiae: ex Officina Bernhardi Tauchnitz, 1879-1881. Ed. anastatice repetita, Lipsiae: Tauchnitz, 1928).

[26] C. 28, C. XXXII, q. 7; cf. also *Glossa Ordinaria* s. v. *Usque adeo .* casus: "dicitur his quod manet . . . vinculum coniugale, etiamsi divortium interveniat sicut manet character Baptismatis, etsi apostatando a charitate recedat."

Ivo's application of the doctrine of Augustine in the *Nec concubinae ad tempus* was slightly paraphrased by Gratian:

"Concubinae ad tempus adhibitae, nec etiamsi causa filiorum
concumbant, iustum faciunt concubinatum suum. IV Pars
[Gratian.] Sic econtrario datur intellegi de his qui coniugali
affectu sibi copulantur, quod etsi non causa procreandorum
filiorum, sed explendi libidinis conveniunt, non ideo fornicarii,
sed coniuges appellantur." [27]

The application of the threefold blessing of marriage to the
marriage of Our Lady and St. Joseph was also repeated.[28]

The *Decretum* of Gratian was the subject of much commentary.
The standard work of commentary, in the form of glosses around
the text, was the *Glossa Ordinaria,* the work of Joannes Teutonicus,
which was completed about 1215-16. This was amended by Bartholomaeus Brixiensis (c. 1240). In commenting on the *Solet quaeri,*
the Glossa explained that consent had to be regarded as essential to
any marriage contract.[29]

This consent to the marriage contract had to extend to an indissoluble union; only that contract which would endure until death
could be called a marriage, for the *Glossa* stated: *"matrimonium
non potest ad tempus contrahi"*.[30]

The scholastics of the twelfth century were still, like their predecessors, groping for an understanding of the nature of the
"sacramentum" in marriage. There was no unanimity of thought
on all points, so that, for instance, Gandulphus (c. 1170) recognized
only two blessings of marriage, those of fidelity and off-spring.[31]

---

[27] C. 5, C. XXXII, q. 2.
[28] C. 5, C. XXVII, q. 2.
[29] *Glossa Ordinaria,* ad c. 6. C. XXXII, q. 2: ". . . ea fide media, ut nec ille
cum altera nec illa cum altero id faciant (i.e. copulantur) . . . dum tamen hoc
agant ut matrimonium contrahant." — *Decretum Gratiani emendatum et notationibus illustratum, una cum glossis, Gregorii XIII Pont. Max. jussu editum*
(3 vols., Taurini, 1588)
[30] *Glossa Ordinaria, loc. cit.;* cf. also *Glossa Ord.* ad c. 10, C. XXVII, q. 2, s. v.
sacramentum; "Sacramentum . . . id est, inseparabilitas. Ad tempus enim non
potest contrahi matrimonium." See also *Glossa Ord.* ad c. 6. C. XXXII, q. 2, s. v.
utrumque: "qui volunt usque ad mortem commanere."
[31] *Glossa Ord.* ad c. 10, C. XXVII, q. 2, s.v. *omne:* "Gandulphus dixit duo
esse tantum bona matrimonii, scilicet fidem et prolem, sed ipsum sacramentum
non esse bonum matrimonii nisi intransitive intelligatur, id est bonum quod est
matrimonium quia sacramentum matrimonii nihil aliud est quam ipsum
sacramentum."

This interpretation by Gandulphus arose from a misunderstanding of the term *"sacramentum"*; the blessing of the sacrament was not the sacrament itself, as St. Augustine had noted, but a special firmness of the bond in a Christian marriage.[32]

At the end of the twelfth century, the end of the period of the Decretists, one important development in the canonical treatment of the matter of indissolubility can be noted in the teaching of Huguccio (+ 1210), the most influential canonical writer of his time.[33] Huguccio taught that any injected condition against the substantial elements of matrimonial contract rendered it invalid. This was so, whether the contrary condition is expressed or not, and even if its existence could not be proved in the external forum. A condition which, when attached to the contract, ran counter to the essential note of indissolubility made that contract invalid.[34]

There was still, at that time, much disagreement among the canonists on the consequences of a conditional consent. This was due in great part to the disparities between the legislation itself and the canonical doctrine. Accordingly, a radical clarification of this legislation regarding conditions in the marriage contract was still called for.[35]

---

[32] *De Bono Conjugali*, Cap. VII—*CSEL*, XXXXI, 197.

[33] In the *Summa super Decretis* (1188-90) Huguccio treated the *Decretum* of Gratian so thoroughly that he is considered to have left no question on Gratian unanswered. Cf. Kuttner, "Bernardus Compostellanus Antiquus" in *Traditio: Studies in Ancient and Medieval History, Thought and Religion*, (Cosmopolitan Science and Art Service Co., Inc., New York, 1943—), I (1943), 283-4.

[34] "Quid si neuter hoc exprimat, scilicet quod velit ad tempus contrahere vel quamdiu voluerit . . . numquid est matrimonium? Respondet Huguccio: Notavit C. XXXII, q. 2, c. solet quaeri . . . quod quidam dicunt adiectionem temporis tunc demum matrimonium impedire, si exprimatur in ipso contractu, aliter non; sed ipse dicit, quod sive exprimatur, sive non, non est matrimonium, licet probari non possit quando non est expressum a contrahentibus, sicut dicitur quod non est matrimonium, ubi non est consensus animorum, licet verbo dicunt simul se consentire."—*Summa Sancti Raymundi* (Veronae, 1744), Lib. IV, c. VII, *Quae Bona Matrimonii*.

[35] Cf. Bartholomew Timlin, *Conditional Matrimonial Consent*, The Catholic University of America Canon Law Studies, n. 89 (Washington, D.C.: The Catholic University of America, 1934), pp. 41-42.

CHAPTER II

THE PERFECTING OF THE CANONICAL DOCTRINE

Article I. Gregory IX and the Early Decretalists

On September 5, 1234, with the promulgation of the Bull *Rex Pacificus,* Pope Gregory IX (1227-1241) introduced a comprehensive collection of decretal law, prepared by St. Raymond of Pennafort. Among the new decretals in the collection there appeared a title on conditional consent with reference to the marriage contract: *De Conditionibus Appositis in Matrimonio et Aliis Contractibus.* Giving examples of conditions which were opposed to each of the three blessings of marriage, the Pope declared that the injection of such conditions which exclude a substantial element of marriage rendered such a contract invalid, regardless of the favor that marriage otherwise enjoyed. Because of this favor, however, any other conditions not opposed to the substance of marriage, even though wrongfully injected into the contract, would be considered as not having been injected at all.

> Si conditiones contra substantiam coniugii inserantur, puta, si alter dicat alteri: 'contraho tecum, si generationem prolis evites' vel 'donec inveniam aliam honore vel facultatibus digniorem' aut 'si pro quaestu adulterandam te tradas', matrimonialis contractus, quantumcumque sit favorabilis, caret effectu; licet aliae conditiones appositae in matrimonio, si turpes aut impossibiles fuerint, debeant propter eius favorem pro non adiectis haberi.[1]

Gregory soon had an opportunity to apply this teaching. Within a year a case was proposed to the Holy See regarding an abuse of the marriage contract, in that consent was given according to the local custom, namely that the woman was to be retained only if she pleased the husband; otherwise she was to be returned to her parents. In a letter to the Procurator of the Dominicans at Treviso, Gregory reprobated such a custom, since the condition attached to the contract was contrary to a substantial element of marriage, indissolubility.[2]

---

[1] C. 7, X, *de conditionibus appositis in desponsatione vel in aliis contractibus,* IV, 5; Potthast, *Regesta Pontificum Romanorum, inde ab anno post Christum natum MCXVIII ad annum MCCCIV* (2 vols., Berolini, 1874-75), n. 9664 (hereafter cited *Potthast*).

[2] "Cum in Sclavoniae partibus consuetudinem pessimam, quae dicenda est verius corruptela, esse proponas, iuxta quam sub ea conditione mulier coniugitur viro,

With this decretal of Pope Gregory much inaccuracy was dissipated; it became definitely established that any condition in the marriage contract against the essence of an indissoluble union rendered that contract null and void. Thus, in the revision of the *Apparatus* of the *Glossa Ordinaria,* made about 1240 by Bartholomaeus of Brescia, one finds the *Solet quaeri* re-evaluated according to the teachings of the *Si Conditiones.*[3]

As the commentary of Joannes Teutonicus had been accepted as the *Glossa Ordinaria* for the *Decretum* of Gratian, so the commentary of Bernard of Parma (d. 1266) became the *Glossa Ordinaria* for the Decretals. Bernard, in his commentary, gave full consideration to the various types of conditions. These he divided as follows: licit conditions, admitted by law; honorable conditions which are according to the substance of marriage; unworthy and evil conditions, some of which are against the substance of marriage itself, so that a marriage contract with such a condition attached is invalid. Any such evil conditions which are attached to the contract against one of the essential blessings of marriage nullify that contract.[4]

St. Raymond of Pennafort (d. 1275), in addition to his work on the Decretals, also prepared his *Summa,* a commentary on the same matters. In the fourth book of the *Summa, Quae Bona Matrimonii,* there was a clear treatment of the blessing of the sacrament and of

si sibi placuerit in Matrimonio retinenda, alioquin reddenda parentibus sine mutilatione, vel fractione membrorum; Nos tibi super hoc propter animarum periculum consilium postulanti, taliter respondemus, quod cum contra substantiam Matrimonii talis conditio inseratur, pro eo quod ad tempus nec debet nec potest matrimonium celebrari, sic contrahentes monendi sunt propense et hortandi, ut de novo inter se matrimonialiter contrahant secundum formam Ecclesiae consuetam; quod si forte non fecerint, denuntiari debet eisdem, quod non matrimonia sed contubernia sunt potius inter eos, nec legitime sed fornicarie commiscentur." —*Bullarium Ordinis Praedicatorum* (ed. a T. Ripall, recognitum a A. Bremond, 8 vols., Romae, 1729-40), I, p. 76, n. CXXX, *"Cum in Sclavoniae";* Potthast, n. 9942.

[3] "...si enim apponitur inhonesta conditio, quae est contra naturam matrimonii, matrimonium non tenet, ut si hoc modo dicatur: 'contraho tecum usque ad tres annos'." — *Glossa Ordinaria,* ad c. 6, C. XXXII, q. 2, s.v. *nolint.*

[4] "Sic videtur quod omnis conditio quae est contra naturam contractus, ipsum impediat, si apponatur. Et haec est ratio, cum tria debeant esse bona matrimonii, saltem quoad propositum: scilicet: fides, proles et sacramentum. Per illas tres conditiones extinguuntur illa tria bona, quae in quolibet matrimonio necessario requiruntur, aliter non erit matrimonium, ut hic patet." — *Glossa Ordinaria,* ad c. 7, X, *de conditionibus appositis etc.,* IV, 5, s.v. *si conditiones.*

the conditions wrongfully placed against it. Granting the possibility of physical separation of husband and wife for just cause, Raymond rejected any possible dissolution of the bond of marriage for the faithful, apart from entrance into religion before the consummation of that marriage union. Once a marriage had been consummated, only the death of one of the parties could dissolve the bond established.[5]

A marriage contract will be valid, according to St. Raymond, if, at the time of making the contract, the parties intend to observe the essential elements of marriage included in the three blessings of offspring, fidelity and the sacrament, even though they may later act in a contrary fashion. Similarly, despite the fact that the contracting parties did not think of the threefold blessings at all, the contract will be a valid one, as long as they did not place a contrary condition or agreement.[6]

Following the teachings of Huggucio, Raymond held that any contrary condition, to be such, had to be made part of the contract at the time of its making, though there was no need of its being expressed in the contract. He also quoted Huggucio's authority regarding the invalidity of a temporary contract.[7] This perpetuity of a marriage, Raymond pointed out, was inseparable from the marriage, so that the third blessing, that of the sacrament, had always to be actually present.[8]

Hostiensis (Henricus de Segusio, Cardinal of Ostia) supported

---

[5] "Bona matrimonii principaliter sunt tria: fides, proles, sacramentum. In sacramento attenditur ut coniugium non separetur; licet enim separatio corporalis fiat interdum causa fornicationis vel ex communi consensu causa orationis seu religionis, sacramentalis separatio tamen non potest fieri; nisi quum desinit esse vinculum matrimonii, quod inter fideles numquam contingit, nisi per ingressum religionis, ante copulam carnis, vel post carnalem copulam per mortem utriusque vel alterius coniugum." — *Summa Sancti Raymundi,* Lib. IV, *Quae Bona Matrimonii,* Tit. II, VII.

[6] "....si tempore contractus intendant ista servare, licet postea mutatis voluntatibus contrarium faciant, tenet nihilominus matrimonium. Idem dico, si nihil cogitant de istis bonis, sufficit enim quod non apponant conditionem vel pactum, ut contra faciant." — *Summa Sancti Raymundi, loc. cit.*

[7] "De sacramento dicitur quod semper exigitur, adeo quod si contrahant aliqui eo animo ut separentur aliquando, non fit ibi matrimonium, quia videntur contrahere ad tempus." — *Summa Sancti Raymundi, loc. cit.*

[8] "Patet ex praemissis quod prima duo bona quandoque comitantur matrimonium, quandoque non; tertium, vero, inseparabiliter adhaeret, quamdiu durat matrimonium." — *Summa Sancti Raymundi, olc. cit.*

these teachings in his *Summa Aurea* (c. 1253). The third blessing of marriage, the blessing of the sacrament, had to be present, and the parties to the contract had to advert expressly to the matter of indissolubility. If they did not they failed to set up any obligation by means of a mutual agreement. To affect the validity of the contract, however, any condition had to exist at the time of the making of the contract, regardless of any subsequent change of mind.[9]

In most of these matters there was agreement among the leading authors of the time. There was one field of disagreement; namely, on the question whether sexual intercourse following upon a conditional marriage consent could *ipso facto* validate the contract, in that equivalently it was a retraction of the condition and a formulation of actual consent (*"consensus de praesenti"*). This disagreement was occasioned by a declaration of Pope Innocent III, first included in the Third Compilation and later incorporated in the Decretals:

> . . . consultationi tuae taliter respondemus, quod cum liquido constet per confessionem tam viri quam mulieris, quod post contracta sponsalia, carnalis est inter eos copula subsecuta; pro matrimonio, quod praesumendum est vehementer, quia videtur a conditione interposita recessisse.[10]

St. Raymond had upheld this stand of the Pontiff,[11] but Hostiensis disagreed, although he recognized that his opinion was opposed to what the Pope had said.[12]

By the end of this period, then, certain doctrines had become clearly defined and universally accepted: the triple blessing of marriage; the meaning of the blessing of the sacrament, namely, the indissolubility of the bond in the marriage of baptized persons, once that marriage had been consummated. The invalidating effect

---

[9] *Summa Aurea (Venetiis,* 1570), Lib. IV, *De Matrimonio: "Et Quare"*, p. 327, n. 19.

[10] Cf. c. 6, X, *de conditionibus appositis etc.,* IV, 5; *Compilatio Tertia,* c. 1, IV, 4, in Antonius Augustinus, *Quinque Compilationes Antiquae* (Ilerdae, 1576), (hereafter cited Augustinus).

[11] *Summa Sancti Raymundi,* Lib. IV, Tit. 4, *De Impedimento Conditionis,* p. 484.

[12] "Et sic potest apparere etiam in foro contentioso, quod carnalis copula non semper probat matrimonium, quod est contra id quod dicit Papa." — *Commentaria in Quinque Decretalium Libros* (5 vols. in 3, Venetiis, 1581), c. 7, *de conditionibus appositis,* IV, s.v. *si conditiones,* p. 17.

of a condition contrary to the element of perpetuity was also accepted by all canonists.

There was no such unanimity on whether such a condition had to be expressed in word or act. The more common opinion contended that the condition had to be agreed on by the parties. If the condition was unilateral only, the marriage was generally held to be valid, since it was then to be understood that the other party, by keeping silent or by actually opposing it, forced the revocation of the condition.[13] This matter remained a subject of contention among the canonical writers during the period of the decretalists from the fourteenth to the sixteenth century.

ARTICLE II. DECRETALISTS OF THE 14TH AND 15TH CENTURY

Joannes Andreae (1270-1348), one of the ablest commentators of the 14th century, held that not even the Supreme Pontiff could render possible the contracting of a valid marriage on a temporary basis. A contract thus conceived and projected ran counter to the very nature of a marital union.[14]

In the *Additiones* to the *Summa Aurea* of Hostiensis [15] this doctrine was accept and followed by another commentator of this period who was cited as Martinus.[16]

---

[13] This dispute seemed to arise from the fact that in all the documents cited as sources there was the expression *"si alter dicat alteri"* and the examples given all indicate that one party was expressly contracting with the other according to the condition. Cf. c. 7, X, *de conditionibus appositis etc.,* IV, 5.

[14] "An ex causa posset Papa dispensative concedere quod matrimonium contraheretur duraturum solum usque quo filius masculus ex matrimonio haberetur. Allegatur quod non: propter duo inconvenientia: primum, quod contraheretur ad tempus, secundum quod dissolveretur iam consummatum. Conditio quae facit matrimonium temporale vitiat contractum, quia contra eius naturam." —*Commentarium in Sextum Decretalium de Regulis Iuris,* Regula L: *"Actus legitimi conditionem non recipiunt neque diem"* (hereafter cited *Regulae Iuris*).

[15] *Summa Aurea,* Lib. IV, *De Matrimonio, Additiones,* p. 328.

[16] It is uncertain who this Martinus was. In the Venice edition (1570) of the *Summa Aurea,* he was identified in the editor's foreword (*Jurisprudentiae Studiosis Bibliopola*) as the author of an alphabetical *Summa,* a man skilled in both canon and civil law . . . *"ordine Franciscanus, jure Abbas dictus, patrum siquidem lacernatorum numero cooptatus merito."* This foreword provides many discrepancies in the light of all the possible authors listed under the name Martinus in the present histories dealing with canon law sources. It is the suggestion of Dr. Stephan Kuttner, *viva voce,* that this might be a mistake in the text, and that the commentary ascribed to Martinus belongs rather to Monaldus. There is much to recommend this suggestion: Monaldus was a Franciscan who died in either 1282 or 1288-9; he belongs therefore to this time. He was skilled in civil law. He wrote a *Summa Iuris "sub singulis litteris alphabeticis,"* which begins

Nicholaus de Tudeschis (1386-1453), called Panormitanus, clarified many of the problems regarding conditions contrary to the substance of marriage. He asserted that the examples given by Gregory IX did not constitute a complete list; many other examples could have been given.[17] Although Panormitanus recognized the distinction between suspensive and resolvent conditions, he held that a condition contrary to the substance of marriage was not only suspensive, but also resolvent, and, for that very reason, such a condition invalidated the marriage.[18] In truth, such a condition could not properly be resolvent in character, since there never was a marriage to which a resolving was applicable. The reason for this was evident: the condition in question served to annihilate the very substance, without which the contract itself could not be made.[19]

In the dispute whether, for the invalidation of the contract, a condition contrary to the indissolubility had to be placed by way of mutual agreement of the parties, those authors who postulated such a mutual agreement as necessary based their arguments on the words of the *Si conditiones*: *"si alter dicat alteri"*. If only one party invoked such a contrary condition, it was held as not invoked (*non adiecta*), and the marriage was deemed valid.

Innocent IV had held that both parties had to agree to the condition before an invalidation could result, and that, if one of the parties opposed the condition or remained silent, the marriage was

---

with the words: *"Abbas debet esse vel fieri sacerdos . . .,"* which could account for the name *Abbas* attributed to the author. (Cf. von Schulte, *Die Geschichte der Quellen und Literatur des canonischen Rechts, von Papst Gregor IX. bis zum Concil von Trient* (Stuttgart: Enke, 1877), § 100, pp. 414-418.

[17] "Licet textus hic ponat tria exempla istarum conditionum contra substantiam, tamen multa alia possent reperiri." — Panormitanus, *Commentaria in Quinque Libros Decretalium* (5 vols. in 7, Venetiis, 1588), Lib. IV, Cap. 7, *de conditionibus appositis,* s.v. *si conditiones,* p. 33 (hereafter cited *Commentaria*).

[18] "Conditio contra substantiam impedit matrimonium nedum quoniam est conditio suspendens sed est resolvens, licet aliqui ex male ad hoc non advertant; putentes quod ex quo semel matrimonium tenuit, conditio resolvens debet haberi pro non adiecta, quod est falsum, ut hic vides." — *Commentaria, loc. cit.*

[19] "Nunquam fuit matrimonium et sic proprie non potest dici resolvens . . . nam remota substantia alicuius, removetur et ipse actus, nam sine substantia nihil potest subsistere." — *Commentaria, loc. cit.*

to be considered valid.[20] Panormitanus, when commenting on this teaching of Innocent IV, submitted this reason for the latter's doctrine:

> Innocentius intellexit textus quando uterque consensit conditioni. Si autem alter contradixit, tenet matrimonium, si fuit processus ad consummationem ipsius; idem dicit favore matrimonii, si alter tacuit et sic tacendo habetur pro contradicente . . . quod in aliis actibus tacens videatur consentire contractui secundum protestationem alterius, licet protestatio sit onerosa et odiosa.[21]

This teaching was based on a comparison with other legitimate acts, such as elections,[22] in which one who, by his silence, would suffer some prejudice to his rights, had the obligation either to protest or else to suffer the prejudice.[23]

At the end of the 15th century there appeared the work of Sylvester Mozzolini (Prierias) (1456-1523), the *Summa Sylvestrina*, which was not a commentary, but a *Summa* for confessors. This work summed up the doctrine of the pre-Tridentine period. Its author inclined rather to the opinion which minimized the number of invalidating conditions in a marriage contract. From his summary, one may note the status of the doctrine before the Council of Trent.

The instrumental cause of marriage is the consent expressed by words or other signs, or even in consequence of the lack of any contradiction to the contract. No consent dealing with the future could effect the contract, even if intercourse followed, and a temporary consent was an invalid consent. Further, the three blessings of marriage were so essential that any condition contrary to any of them rendered the marriage null. When it could not be proved, however, that such a condition had been made, and later the mar-

---

[20] "Melius diceret pacta. Nisi ambo consentiant, non impeditur matrimonium. Si . . . alius contradicat, matrimonium est; sed si taceat, idem; quia praesumitur contradicere in favorem matrimonii." — Innocentius IV, *Commentaria in V Libros Decretalium* (Venetiis, 1570), IV, VII, *de condittionibus appositis in desponsatione*, p. 562.

[21] *Commentaria, loc. cit.*

[22] C. 50, X *de electione et electi potestate*, I, 6; Potthast, n. 8152.

[23] *Commentaria*, Lib. I, Cap. 50, *de electione et electi potestate*, s.v. *cumana*, p. 459.

riage became consummated, the judgement in such a case was to favor the validity of the marriage. The same judgement was applicable if only one of the contracting parties attached the condition and the other either opposed it or remained silent.[24] Thus Prierias accepted as his own the opinion of Innocent III and of Panormitanus, namely that silence on the side of one of the parties was to be considered as the equivalent of opposition to an attached condition contrary to the nature of marriage. The other party was thereby deemed to have abandoned his previously invoked conditions. This interpretation he held as applicable for both the external and the internal forum.[25]

Between the general tenets of the early decretists and decretalists and the views expressed by Prierias, there was much room for a greater clarification of the issues. This was in great part to come in canonical commentary subsequent to the doctrine established in the Council of Trent.

ARTICLE III. DOCTRINE OF THE COUNCIL OF TRENT AND SUBSEQUENT CANONICAL COMMENTARY

A. THE DOCTRINE OF THE COUNCIL OF TRENT

The Council of Trent (1545-1563), the nineteenth general council, besides defining many points of faith, enacted many disciplinary measures. Although the Fathers of the Council did not enact any specific decrees regarding conditional matrimonial consent or with reference to the exclusion of indissolubility in the marriage contract,

---

[24] "Causa instrumentalis est consensus expressus per verba vel nutus vel alia signa vel per non contradicere in desponsatione. Et si exprimatur consensus per verba de futuro, non facit matrimonium . . . imo nec addita copula carnali . . . nec similiter facit matrimonium consensus ad tempus . . Et haec tria (bona) adeo sunt substantialia coniugio quod conditio contra aliquod eorum apposita vitiat contractum matrimonii." — *Summa Sylvestrina* (Venetiis, 1601), Pars II. *Matrimonium*, I, p. 133.

"Tamen, si postea talis conditio remittatur et sequatur copula carnalis, iudicabitur pro matrimonio. Et similiter pro matrimonio iudicabitur si alter tantum coniugum eam ponit et reliquus contradicit aut tacet." — *Op. cit.*, p. 138.

"In conditionem uterque expresse consentiat; si aliter . etiam si taceat, erit matrimonium purum et teneret matrimonium, quamvis conditio esset contra substantiam eius." — *Op. cit.*, p. 140.

[25] "Et idem dicit favore matrimonii si alter tacuit et sic tacens habebitur pro contradicente . . . Videtur recessum a conditione . . . Ista non solum sunt vera quoad forum contentiosum, sed etiam in foro animae." — *Op. cit., Matrimonium*, IV, p. 142.

they did emphasize the indissoluble and perpetual nature of that contract.[26] Furthermore, in the decree on the new form for the manifesting of the consent, which aimed at doing away with clandestine marriages, the Council seemed to strike at any sort of a conditional marriage.[27]

No new legislation on the matter was necessary for substantive law; the nullifying laws incorporated in Gregory's Decretal were to remain in force. Post-Tridentine authors, however, in both the theological and the canonical fields, were to develop that teaching more completely in the light of the decrees of the Council of Trent. At this stage of jurisprudential development, there were certain matters held as common doctrine, but there were also three distinct areas of dispute. In the post-Tridentine development one notes a gradual clarification in these disputed matters.

B. The *Status Quaestionis* at the Time

1. Accepted Common Doctrine

All authors after Panormitanus agreed that the list of conditions against the substance of the contract as furnished by Gregory IX in his Decretal: *"si generationem prolis evites," "donec inveniam aliam honore vel facultatibus digniorem,"* and *"si pro quaestu adulterandam te tradas,"*[28] served simply to present examples of nullifying conditions, and did not comprise in itself a complete enumeration of all the possible contrary conditions.[29] Another point agreed on was that any true condition placed against an indissoluble union nullified the marriage contract.[30] It was similarly agreed that it did not

[26] *Canones et Decreta Concilii Tridentini* (editio Neapolitana Josephi Palella, Neapoli, 1858), Sessio XXIV, *De Reformatione Matrimonii*, p. 215; Canon V and Canon VII, *ibid.*

[27] Ayrinhac-Lydon, *Marriage Legislation in the New Code of Canon Law,* (revised ed., New York: Benziger Brothers, 1949), p. 222; cf. also: *Canones et Decreta C. Tridentini, Decretum,* Sess. XXIV, *de. ref.,* c. 1.

[28] C. 7, X, *de conditionibus appositis etc.,* IV, 5.

[29] "Tria exempla habes in textu . . . id fecit exempli gratia. Unde idem dicendum in omnibus aliis conditionibus, quae substantiae matrimoni adversantur."— Fagnanus, *Commentaria in V Libros Decretalium* (Venetiis, 1709), Lib. IV, *De Conditionibus Appositis,* p. 42, n. 2 (hereafter cited *Commentaria*); cf. also Covarruvias y Leyva, *Omnia Opera* (2 vols., Coloniae Allobrogum, 1679), *De Matrimonio,* Pars II, Cap. 3, § 1, *De Conditionibus Appositis,* p. 184, n. 21 (hereafter cited *De Matrimonio*).

[30] "Conditio contraria substantiae matrimonii aut bonis eius illud irritum reddit." — Sanchez, *De Sancto Matrimonii Sacramento Tomi Tres* (10 libri in 3

matter whether these conditions were of a resolvent or of a suspensive character; if they militated against the very substance of marriage they rendered that marriage contract null.[31] Authors likewise agreed on the fact that even dishonorable or impossible conditions against the substance of marriage or its essential attribute of indissolubility, rather than being regarded as not attached to the contract, were held simply to invalidate it.[32]

2. Matters of Dispute

The essential doctrine on the invalidating effect of a condition placed against the indissolubility of the marriage contract, which is the proper study of this dissertation, was thus clearly established by the end of the 16th century. There were still under discussion certain questions relating to the contrary condition. These were based on the varying interpretations of passages in the *Decretum* of Gratian and in the Decretals of Gregory IX. In examining the decretal *"Si conditiones"* [33] in the light of the distinctions drawn from the Roman Law, the commentators disagreed on what kinds of conditions had invalidating effects.

Another source of disagreement was the text of St. Augustine drawn from his *De Nuptiis et Concupicentia*, Lib. I, c. 15, and reproduced in the *Decretum* of Gratian in the chapter *"Aliquando"*[34] from which many commentators inferred that, with reference to the contrary condition, there had to be an express agreement be-

---

vols., Venetiis, 1726), Vol. I. Lib. V, *De Consensu Conditionato*, Disp. IX, n. 3, p. 314 (hereafter cited *De Matrimonii Sacramento*). Cf. also: Covarruvias, *De Matrimonio*, ibid., p. 181, n. 1; Navarrus, *Omnia Opera in VI Tomos Distributa* (Venetiis, 1618), Vol. I, *De Matrimonii Impedimentis Impedientibus*, Cap. XXII, n. 62, p. 369 (hereafter cited *De Matrimonii Impedimentis*).

[31] "... sicut non tenet matrimonium contractum sub conditione suspensiva.... ita nec tenet, si contractus fuerit sub conditione resolutiva . . . quia etsi conditio sit resolutiva, tamen vim operatur quod suspensiva." — Fagnanus, *ibid.*, nn. 6-7.

[32] "Tandem dubitatur de conditione impossibili contraria substantiae matrimonii. an reiicienda sit vel potius annullat matrimonium? Non reiici, sed annullare matrimonium . . quia talis conditio cum tollat matrimonii substantiam excludit consensum absque quo matrimonium consistere nequit." — Sanchez, *De Matrimonii Sacramento*, Lib. V, Disp. IV, n. 19, p. 303. Cf. also De Lugo, *Omnia Opera* (Venetiis, 1718), *Disputationes de Justitia et Jure*, Vol. II, Disp. XXII, *De Contractibus in genere*, Sec. XIII, n. 347, p. 54 (hereafter cited *De Justitia et Jure*); Sanchez (*loc. cit.*) cited many of his contemporaries and predecessors as in agreement with himself.

[33] C. 7, X, *de conditionibus appositis etc.*, IV, 5.

[34] C. 8, C. XXXII, q. 2.

tween the two parties; otherwise the marriage was to be honored as valid.

The third passage affording matter for dispute was the *"Per tuas nobis"* of Pope Innocent III (1198-1216),[35] which engendered the teaching of many that the parties' subsequent act of carnal intercourse indicated that the previously invoked condition had been withdrawn, and that as a consequence the marriage was to be considered a valid one.

In the centuries after the Council of Trent, the following questions were considered by almost all canonical commentators: the types of invalidating conditions, the *"deductio conditionis in pactum"* and the effect of the *"copula secuta"* on a marriage entered into with a condition contrary to the substance of the contract. Upon the resolution of these difficulties there could emerge the modern doctrine on the invalidating character of conditions contrary to the perpetuity of the marriage bond.

3. CLARIFICATION OF THESE ISSUES

It may be useful to explain the background of two of the issues in dispute: the types of conditions and the meaning of the *"deductio conditionis in pactum."*

a. *Types of Conditions*

The *Glossa Ordinaria* to the *Decretum* of Gratian distinguished various types of conditions:

> Conditio quaedam est honesta, quaedam inhonesta, sive impossibilis. Est autem honesta duplex et est duplex inhonesta. Quaedam enim conditio est de natura matrimonii, quaedam non. Si ergo conditio honesta, quae non est de natura matrimonii, apponatur matrimonio, tenet matrimonium . . . Est alia honesta conditio quae adhaeret naturae matrimonii . . . Similiter inhonesta duplex est; si enim apponitur inhonesta conditio, quae est contra naturam matrimonii, matrimonium non tenet . . . Est et alia inhonesta conditio, quae non est contra naturam matrimonii.[36]

To these *"conditiones de futuro"* of the *Glossa,* Vincentius Hispanus

---

[35] C. 6, X, *de conditionibus appositis etc.,* IV, 5; *Augustinus, Compilatio IIIa,* c. 1, IV, 4.

[36] *Glossa Ordinaria,* ad c. 6, C. XXXII, q. 2, s.v. *nolint.*

(d. 1248), who wrote the *Apparatus* to the *Compilatio III a,* added *"conditiones de praesenti et de praeterito"* [37] and *"impossibilis de iure"* or *"impossibilis ex natura."* [38]

These types of conditions were studied by the authors in the light of Roman Law, which, according to the common opinion, did not recognize a specifically resolvent condition, but only a suspensive one.[39] Since the condition delineated by Gregory, *"donec aliam inveniam"*, was not of a suspensive but of a resolvent character, this latter note or element also had to be accommodated within the general concept of a conditional consent.

One accordingly finds the following kinds of conditions discussed by the authors: the *conditio de praeterito, de praesenti* and *de futuro,* depending on whether the circumstance on which the validity of the obligation of a lawful act was to depend was associated with the past, the present or the future; the *conditio possibilis,* when the circumstance, according to the natural order of things, existed either necessarily (*conditio necessaria*) or purely in some contingent fashion (*conditio contingens*); the *conditio impossibilis,* when the circumstance, in the natural order of things, either absolutely or at least physically or morally transcended all powers available for its realization or verification; the *conditio honesta,* which conformed to human and divine laws and the *conditio turpis,* which was opposed to these laws. One could further think of a condition, whether honorable (*honesta*) or dishonorable (*turpis*), which was opposed to the substance of the lawful act (*conditio substantiae repugnans*) or which in no way affected it (*conditio substantiae non repugnans*). Finally, there was the *conditio suspensiva,* which held in abeyance the validity of the act until some future and uncertain event became verified and the *conditio resolutiva,* which, without suspending the validity of the act, had the effect, at a later time when the

[37] Augustinus, *Compilatio IIIa,* ad c. 1, IV, 4, s.v. *videlicet pater.*

[38] Augustinus, *ibid.,* s.v. *sub conditione.*

[39] "Peraltro la condizione resolutiva nel diritto romano non vale come vera e propria condizione . . . bensì come convenzione contraria condizionata, cioè un patto di risoluzione o revoca sottoposto a condizione sospensiva. Il negozio principale è 'purum', ma in virtù della convenzione aggiunta 'sub conditione' resolvitur." — Bonfanti, *Instituzioni di Diritto Romano,* (Romae, 1934), § 26, pp. 77-78.

future and uncertain event was realized, of rescinding the act and cancelling out all continued validity for it.[40]

b. *"Deductio Conditionis in Pactum"*

This question had been discussed by the earlier authors,[41] and among them, as in the later common usage, the condition was delineated as *"in pactum deducta."* Authors did not agree on the extension of meaning inherent in this expression. Some considered the expression to imply that both of the parties to the contract had to invoke the condition in the contracting of the marriage; others considered it as implying an agreement between the parties, entered into either at the very celebration of the marriage or even before, as long as it was not later revoked, but entered into in such a way that the existence of the pact could be proved in the external forum.[42] Several authors held that it was not necessary for both parties to agree to the condition; the condition was *"in pactum deducta"* also if one of the parties placed the condition and the other party did not consciously oppose it.[43] For other authors the formula was to be understood in the sense that the condition affected the matrimonial pact or contract, not indeed in the sense that both the parties had to enter into the pact that contemplated the attached condition, but rather in the sense that the contract was to be regarded as conditional, even when only one of the parties had invoked the condition.[44]

In general, the common denominator for all the authors was that a condition *"in pactum deducta"*, in order to be such, had in some way to be susceptible of proof in the external forum.

[40] These definitions, which best describe the various types as they appear in the authors, are taken from Wernz, *Ius Decretalium ad Usum Praelectionum in Scholis Textus Canonici sive Iuris Decretalium* (6 vols. in 10, Romae et Prati, 1898-1914), Vol. IV, *Ius Matrimoniale*, n. 293, pp. 430-31 (hereafter cited *Ius Matrimoniale*).

[41] Cf. *supra*, pp. 16-17.

[42] Cf. Wernz, *Ius Matrimoniale, ibid.*, n. 297.

[43] Cf. Schmalzgrueber, *Ius Ecclesiasticum Universum* (5 vols. in 12, Romae, 1843-45), Lib. IV, Tit. V, n. 48 (hereafter cited *Ius Ecclesiasticum*).

[44] Cf. De Smet, *Tractatus Theologico — Canonicus de Sponsalibus et Matrimonio* (ed. 4, Brugis: Car. Bayaert, 1927), n. 151, nota i, p. 126 (hereafter cited *De Sponsalibus et Matrimonio*). This is the sense in which the expression is understood today.

C. Canonical Commentary After the Council of Trent

1. Types of Conditions

The most influential treatment of the doctrine on marriage after
the Council of Trent was that of Thomas Sanchez, S.J. (1551-1610),
whose doctrine, for the most part, was accepted by subsequent
authors. Much of his teaching, still cited in Rota decisions, is applicable in current canonical commentaries on marriage. For this
reason, it will be referred to in this study in the same manner as
that of modern commentators on the Code.

One of Sanchez' important teachings was his distinction between
a condition invoked against the blessings of offspring and fidelity
and one invoked against the blessing of the sacrament. Although
one could intend to assume the obligations of offspring and fidelity
in a marriage contract, though not intending to fulfill such obligations and thus still contract a valid marriage, the same did not
apply in the presence of a condition against indissolubility. There
had to be the intent both of accepting and of fulfilling the obligation connected with an indissoluble union, if the contract thereto
was to be valid.[45] Therefore, any conditions contrary to indissolubility totally neutralized the substance of marriage and the consent
necessary for the contract.[46] This was so because the substance of
marriage was the consent to a perpetual conjugal union, and nothing
can subsist without its substance. Since the substance of marriage
was destroyed by conditions against perpetuity, the contract thereto
was invalidated. Pope Gregory IX, therefore, was merely declaring
the extant binding law, already established by the natural law.[47]

---

[45] "... aliud esse sentiendum de tribus matrimonii bonis quoad obligationem et
aliud quoad executionem: quoad obligationem, omnia illa sunt de matrimonii essentia . . . quoad executionem et in se ipsis: sic bonum sacramenti, quod est
indissolubile vinculum, est de essentia sacramenti, non autem fides et proles."—
Sanchez, *De Matrimonii Sacramento*, Lib. II, Disp. XXIX, n. 12, p. 116.

[46] "Unde conditiones et pacta, per quae coniuges ad aliquid his contrarium obli-
gantur, tollunt matrimonii substantiam et debitum consensum." — Sanchez, *op.
cit.*, Lib. V, Disp. IX, n. 2, p. 313.

[47] "... sine substantia nihil potest subsistere. Sed substantia matrimonii con-
sistit in consensu ad societatem coniugalem, sub quo tacite includitur consensus
ad perpetuam societatem, ad fidem mutuo servandam, prolemque suscipiendam,
quae sunt tria bona matrimonii. Ergo, conditiones quae his adversantur, destruunt

This same teaching had earlier been proposed by Covarruvias y Leyva (1511-1577),[48] by Martin Azpilcueta, called Navarrus (1493-1586),[49] by Dominic Soto (1494-1560) [50] and by John Paul Lancellotus (1522-1590).[51] It was later adopted by many authors of the seventeenth century.[52]

Contrary to the opinion of some of his predecessors and contemporaries, Sanchez taught that a contrary condition invalidated a marriage contract only when its verification had to look to the future and not when the condition looked to the present. The reason he so concluded was that only that contingency which looked to the future was properly a condition. If it had regard to the present or past, at the time of the contracting, the condition was either verified or not; if it was verified, the marriage was valid, whereas if it was not verified, the marriage was null.[53] In only one case did

substantiam matrimonii, et consequenter ipsum annullabunt." — Sanchez, *op. cit.*, ibid., p. 314.

"....Pontifex dum definivit conditiones has vitiare matrimonium, nil novum statuit, sed quod ius naturae dictabat declaravit." — Sanchez, *op. cit., loc. cit.*

[48] *De Matrimonio*, Cap. III, § 1, n. 1, p. 181, and n. 24, p. 184.

[49] *De Matrimonii Impedimentis*, Cap. XXII, n. 62, p. 369.

[50] *Commentarium in IVum Librum Sententiarum*, Vol. II (Venetiis, 1584), Dist. 29, Ques. II, Art. III, p. 189 (hereafter cited *Commentarium*).

[51] *Institutiones Iuris Canonici* (Venetiis, 1704), Lib. II, Tit. IX, *De Sacramento Matrimonii*, § 4, p. 126 (hereafter cited *Institutiones*). Lancellotus strangely applied the teaching to *four* blessings of marriage: "*fides, proles, evitare peccatum carnis et significare unionem.*" — *Ibid.*, s.v. *consequuntur*, in the *Glossa*.

[52] Cf. Paulus Laymann (1574-1635), *Theologia Moralis* (Venetiis, 1630), Lib. V, *De Sacramentiis*, Tract. V, Cap. VII, n. 11, p. 480 (hereafter cited *De Sacramentis*); Prosper Fagnanus (1598-1678), *Commentaria*, Lib. IV, nn. 6-7, p. 42; Cardinal De Lugo (1583-1660), *De Justitia et Jure*, Disp. XXII, Sec. CIII, n. 348, p. 54; Ernricus Pirhing (1606-1679), *Ius Canonicum in Quinque Libros Decretatium Nova Methodo Explicatum* (ed. novissima, 4 vols., Diligae, 1722), Vol. IV, *De Sponsalibus et Matrimonio*, Tit. V, § 1, Ass. II, p. 65 (hereafter cited *Ius Canonicum*); Gonzalez-Tellez (d. post 1673), *Commentaria Perpetua in Singulos Textus V Librorum Decretalium Gregorii IX*, Vol. IV (Lugduni, 1673), Tit. V, Cap. 7, n. 3, p. 120 and n. 9, p. 124 (hereafter cited *Commentaria*).

[53] "Sed contrarium est verius, nempe solam conditionem contrariam matrimonio illud vitiare, quando est de futuro; secus quando est de praesenti vel praeterito; tunc enim valida est conditio, et, ea existente, matrimonium erit, non autem existente, minime valebit matrimonium. Quia . . . propria conditio non est, nisi quando est de futuro." — Sanchez, *op. cit., ibid.*, n. 2.

Sanchez admit that a condition looking to the present was nevertheless invested with an invalidating force, namely when the parties proposed to contract a marital union for a time only, e.g. for two years, since this would be equivalent to a condition reckoning with the future.[54]

Sanchez did not admit the distinction proposed by his contemporaries, namely that a contrary condition had to be intended as the principal part of the contract or otherwise be rejected as evil. He insisted that such a condition had a nullifying effect in any case, regardless of whether it was of a resolvent or of a suspensive character. Such a condition completely neutralized the substance and the principal blessing of marriage, namely the perpetual and inseparable bond.[55] He also rejected the opinion that suspensive conditions did not nullify the contract, or the opinion that they were to be considered as not attached to the contract. That teaching insisted that suspensive conditions held the formation of the contract in abeyance until the conditions were fulfilled, whereupon the contract of marriage took effect. Sanchez rejected this teaching, contending that also the suspensive condition contrary to the substance of marriage invalidated the contract because it was properly a condition and thus was included in the legislation on contrary conditions.[56] This same opinion had been held by Navarrus,[57] and was later supported by Fagnanus [58] and Pirhing.[59]

There were, moreover, additional points of dispute among the authors in this matter of types of conditions. One of these dealt with the addition of impossible conditions that did not militate against the substance of marriage. According to the common opinion espoused by Sanchez, these were to be considered as not added at

---

[54] Sanchez, *loc. cit.*

[55] ". . . tollit substantiam, ac principale bonum matrimonii, scilicet esse perpetuum ac inseparabile vinculum; ergo, implicat habere legitimatum consensum ad matrimonium requisitum cum ista conditione separabilitatis." — Sanchez, *loc. cit.*

[56] ". . . in utroque casu vitiat matrimonium . . . quia textus loquitur de conditionibus contrariis matrimonio, et proprie est conditio quando suspendit."— Sanchez, *loc. cit.*

[57] Cf. *De Matrimonii Impedimentis*, Cap. XXII, n. 62, p. 369.

[58] Cf. *Commentaria*, Lib. IV, nn. 6-7, p. 42.

[59] Cf. *Ius Canonicum*, Vol. IV, Tit. V, § 1, p. 63.

all, and accordingly the marriage was held to be valid. Just as the civil law rejected conditions impossible of fulfillment in its construction of last wills and testaments, so canon law intended to place the same restriction on the marriage contract. This was the explanation adduced by De Lugo,[60] although he added the warning that any kind of condition which rendered true marital consent impossible had to be considered in the forum of conscience as invested with an invalidating effect.[61]

In discussing these conditions, De Lugo proposed what came to be accepted as a most important factor for deciding between two contrary intentions in the minds of the contracting parties. According to Cardinal De Lugo, two principles were to be kept in mind:

> Quando in contrahente matrimonium dantur duae voluntates contrariae, illam praevalere quae ex se magis efficax est et magis illuminata in ordine ad suum objectum.

> Qui vult celebrare contractum validum, regulariter vult illum celebrare iuxta leges talis contractus.

From these two principles he drew the conclusion that one who attached an impossible condition in the contracting of marriage, if he intended to make a valid contract, wished to make that contract according to the prescriptions of law, and hence wished implicitly to have that impossible condition regarded as not attached, since that was the prescription of law in the matter.[62] Other authors who held this opinion were Fagnanus,[63] Laymann [64] and Pirhing.[65]

Gonzalez-Tellez, however, disagreed with this common opinion, which thus treated impossible conditions in view of the favor which marriage enjoys in behalf of its validity. Many of the adherents of this opinion had based their reasoning on the comparison they in-

---

[60] "Ius canonicum voluisse idem facere circa matrimonium, quod ius civile fecerat circa ultimas voluntates in ordine ad conditiones impossibiles." — *De Justitia et Jure*, Vol. II, Disp. XXII, Sec. XIII, n. 340, p. 53.

[61] "Si enim constet defuisse verum consensum, matrimonium non censebitur validum. In foro conscientiae standum esse intentioni contrahentium sub conditione, qualiscunque conditio sit." — *Op. cit., ibid.*, n. 342.

[62] *Op. cit., ibid.*, nn. 357-359, p. 56.

[63] Cf. *Commentaria*, Lib. IV, nn. 6-7, p. 42.

[64] Cf. *De Sacramentis*, Tract. V, Cap. VII, n. 11, p. 480.

[65] Cf. *Ius Canonicum*, Vol. IV, Tit. V, § 1, p. 63.

voked between conditions attached to contracts and conditions incorporated in wills and testaments. Gonzalez-Tellez pointed out basic differences between the two concepts, notably that in wills and testaments it is to the interest of the testator that his will be carried out, and this the law seeks to do. Furthermore, there are two parties who consent to a contract, whereas in a will the legatees have nothing to do with making the testament and are only passive parties to it.[66] Because of these differences he offered a different doctrine with reference to such impossible conditions. In this marriage contracts did not differ from any other bilateral contracts, so that such conditions nullified the contract for the same reason as in other contracts, namely because no consent was really given. One who attached such a condition seemed to ridicule marriage rather than to consent to it. Gonzalez-Tellez admitted that a union already contracted was to enjoy the favor of law for its validity and, accordingly, should not be dissolved, but to try to establish a marriage in the absence of all consent was a disfavor, and not a favor. He pointed out the fact that no text of law, civil or canon, other than the decretal of Gregory, indicated a total ineffectiveness for attached impossible conditions in the marriage contract, so that the union eventuated as a valid union. He proposed, therefore, that this decretal referred to the contract of espousals, not to the marriage contract.[67] This opinion was followed in a certain sense by Zeger Van

[66] "Placuit prudentibus conditiones impossibiles ultimis dispositionibus adiectas vitiari, non vero eas vitiare: tum quia testatoris interest voluntatem suam adimpleri. Immo et publice interest voluntates defunctorum ratas esse . . . quae ratio cessat in contractibus. Item quia in contractibus sunt duo qui consentiunt et potest ambobus imputari, maxime creditori, quare sub impossibili conditione consensissent. In ultimis dispositionibus nihil est quod legatariis imputetur, quia nihil in testamento faciunt, sed patiuntur." — *Commentaria*, Vol. IV, Tit. V, Cap. VII, n. 6, pp. 121-122.

[67] ". . . nullum discrimen versari inter matrimonium et ceteros contractus; ita ut conditio impossibilis equaliter matrimonium vitiet et ex eadem ratione, videlicet propter defectum consensus, nam qui conditionem impossibilem contractui adiecit, ridere, non consentire videtur . . . Et licet matrimonium iam contractum omni favore dignum sit, ne dissolvatur, tamen ut inducatur matrimonium, ubi nullus consensus coniugalis adest, odium potius quam favor vertitur . . . cum non sit alius textus in utraque lege ex quo deducant vulgo Interpretes, conditiones impossibiles nuptiis adiectas vitiari, matrimonium vero valere, quam praesens con-

Espen (1646-1728), who considered this decretal as referring to conditions added as modes rather than to true conditions. He pointed out:

> "Si enim contrahentes absolute voluissent suum consensum ab eventu conditionis turpis suspendi, non apparet qua ratione posset ante eventum huius conditionis dici verum matrimonium; cum hoc sine consensu contrahentium haberi nequeat."[68]

The opinion of Sanchez, the common opinion, remained the acceptable doctrine, however, and later was incorporated in the law of the Code.[69]

2. DOCTRINE ON THE *Deductio in Pactum*

In his thirteenth Disputation Sanchez reflected the current thought on the *"deductio in pactum"*, and explained the various opinions regarding conditions placed in this form:

I. "Ut vitiet matrimonium, requiri ut apponatur ab utroque contrahente: quare si alter contrahens apponat et alter contradicat, valebit matrimonium."

II. "Si alter contrahens apponat et alter contradicat, tunc non esse matrimonium sed sponsalia."

III. "Si alter contrahens apponat et alter contradicat, non esse sponsalia nec matrimonium."

IV. "Si alter contrahens apponat et alter contradicat, si copula sequatur, est matrimonium; . . . ea non sequente, non est matrimonium."[70]

The first of these opinions Sanchez held to be very probable. He cited as its adherents Innocent IV (d. 1254), Hostiensis (d. 1271),

---

stitutio Gregorii IX . . . dico Gregorium in praesenti textu non agere de conditionibus suspensivis adiectis matrimonio, eius initium impedientibus, quae consensui de praesenti apponi non possunt, sed tantum desponsationi, ut inde non matrimonium, sed sponsalia celebrata conseantur." — *Op. cit., ibid.*, n. 7, p. 122.

[68] *Jus Ecclesiasticum Universum* (Louvanii, 1732), Pt. II, Tit. XII, Cap. IV, n. 18, pp. 189-190, 199.

[69] Canon 1092, 1° — *Codex Iuris Canonici, Pii X Pontificis Maximi iussu digestus, Benedicti Papae XV auctoritate promulgatus, Praefatione, Fontium Annotatione et Indice Analytico-Alphabetico ab Emo Petro Card. Gasparri Auctus* (Romae: Typis Polyglottis Vaticanis, 1917; reimpressio, 1934). Hereafter simply the canon in its proper number will be cited.

[70] *De Matrimonii Sacramento*, Lib. V, Disp. XIII, I, n. 4, p. 317.

Joannes Andreae (d. 1348), Panormitanus (d. 1453) and others. The arguments he proposed for this opinion were two: (1) the *Aliquando* clearly supposes that there is a true marriage when only one consents, since it calls them husband and wife, and (2) one consent is absolute and the other is conditional, but the conditional consent does not vitiate the act and therefore the marriage is valid, since the condition is considered as not added at all.[71]

Sanchez dealt with the arguments for the second opinion in a very summary fashion: *"Nescio cui fundamento innitantur."* [72]

The third opinion Sanchez deemed probable, though in a lesser degree than the first and the fourth. As adherents of this opinion he listed John of Imola (d. 1436), Covarruvias (d. 1577), Antonius Cucchus (d. ca. 1565) and, among the theologians, Adrian (d. 1523) and Peter of Ledesma (d. 1616). Two arguments were offered in substantiation of the opinion that such a contract was neither one of espousals nor of marriage: (1) the difference in consent makes a contract impossible; (2) there is no mutual, absolute giving of bodily rights as is required for a true marriage.[73]

---

[71] "Ex Aliquando, quod clare supponit quando alter tantum consentit, esse verum matrimonium, cum eos viri et uxoris nomine appellat."
"Quia quamvis alter consensus sit purus et alter conditionalis, at ille conditionalis non vitiat actum; ergo valebit matrimonium. Probatur antecedens quia per easdem causas contractus nascitur et dissolvitur. Sed ad matrimonium constituendum est necessarius mutuus consensus, ergo et ad dissolvendum. Cum ergo hic non concurrat alterius consensus in conditionem, ea conditio non vitiat. Si ergo non vitiat: et ex alia parte est turpis, habebitur pro non adiecta, et remanebit consensus purus in matrimonium. Et confirmatur quia conditio nec confert ad contractum matrimonii confirmandum vel infirmandum, nisi ab utraque parte acceptetur. Ergo, cum illa conditio non acceptetur ab utroque, non infirmabit matrimonium, et cum ex alia parte sit turpis, habebitur quasi adiecta non esset."— *Loc. cit.*

[72] *Loc. cit.*

[73] "Diversitas in consensu vitiat contractum. Ut quando alter pure consentit; alter vero sub conditione. Et ratio est manifesta, quia non uniuntur inter se consensus, ex qua unione contractus oritur; ergo, cum in hoc matrimonio inveniatur haec diversitas, erit nullum . . . Ad matrimonium requiritur mutua corporum traditio, at in hoc casu non invenitur; cum alter non absolute tradat corpus, sed sub conditione contraria matrimonii substantiae ac consequenter excludente verum consensum. Ergo, nullo modo est matrimonium." — *Loc. cit.*

In the fourth opinion, the basis for deciding whether the marriage contract was valid or not was to be sought in whether or not a carnal intercourse had followed upon the conditional consent. This opinion was considered by Sanchez as enjoying great probability. Its adherents were Panormitanus (d. 1453), Rosella (ca. 1385-1466), Sylvester (1456-1523), Gregory Lopez (fl. 1550) and Lancellotus (d. 1590). The proof offered for this opinion was that the fact of copula indicated that the party had given up the contrary condition.[74]

The authors were divided on this question. Holding to the opinion that both parties had to agree to the contrary condition if it was to invalidate the contract was Soto: *"Nulla istarum conditionum quidcumque adfert momenti ad matrimonium confirmandum vel infirmandum, nisi ambo contrahentes in illam conditionem consentiant, ut quam unus obtulit, alter accipiat."* [75] Among the commentators who held that an invalidating effect accompanied a condition even when it was attached by simply one of the parties were Gutierrez (ca. 1600), who discarded the first opinion, rejected the second and the fourth completely, but followed the third opinion "tamquam verissimam et probabiliorem," [76] Covarruvias [77] and De Lugo.[78]

Lancellotus agreed with Panormitanus that the consent of both parties had to be involved, for: *"si alter vel contradicit vel etiam tacuit, tenet matrimonium, si sit processum ad consummationem . . . Item . . . ut impediant matrimonium, debent deduci in pactum*

---

[74] "Ex eo quod alter tacet vel contradicat, non videtur a conditione recessum, cum mutatio animae praesumi non soleat, nisi facto vel verbo declaretur. Ergo, cum non adest copula, non videtur recedi a conditione, at cum adest, eo ipso videtur a conditione recedi et matrimonium erit purum." — *Loc. cit.*

[75] *Commentarium*, Vol. II, Dist. 29, Q. II, Art. I, p. 180.

[76] Gutierrez, *Iurisconsulti Praeclarissimi Hispani Canonicarum Quaestionum Utriusque Fori* (Nurembergae, 1647), III *Tractatus De Matrimonio, De Conditionibus Contra Substantiam Matrimonii*, n. 18, pp. 245-246 (hereafter cited *Tractatus de Matrimonio*).

[77] *De Matrimonio*, Cap. III, § b, nn. 14-16, p. 183.

[78] "Matrimonium est nullum, si fiat sub conditione quae sit contra eius substantiam . . . licet id non deducat in pactum externum, matrimonium etiam est nullum." — *De Sacramentis in Genere*, Vol. V, (*Omnia Opera*, Venetiis, 1718), Disp. VIII, Sec. VIII, nn. 127-130, p. 403.

expressum; secus, si sit propositum in mente retentum." [79]

In his treatment of the *"conditio in pactum deducta"* Cardinal De Lugo developed what was to be a most important distinction in the later case solutions by Benedict XIV, and in the subsequent decisions of the Rota and of the Sacred Congregation of the Council, one which was finally to be incorporated in the Code.[80] He pointed out the difference between antecedent error, which is a speculative error about the dissolubility of the marriage bond, and a concomitant condition or intention of excluding that bond in its perpetual nature from the marriage contract. A simple error was without invalidating effect, unless it entered the contract as a condition or as an intention against the indissoluble bond.

"Si contrahentes ignorabant omnino an vinculum istud esset perpetuum, vel si credebant etiam dissolubile, sed non limitarunt suam intentionem tempore contractus ad eam existimationem, sed habuerunt voluntatem generalem contrahendi matrimonium validum, ita ut illa ignorantia, vel existimatio, se habeat concomitanter cum etiam sine illa aeque contraherent; tunc matrimonium videtur validum et observandum. Concludo ergo errorem illum tunc vitiare matrimonium, quando ex illo contrahens limitat suam intentionem sive per pactum exterius . . . ad quod sufficit vel saltem alterum conjugum limitare suam intentionem ut matrimonium sit nullum . . . Quando vero error ille est concomitans nec ideo contrahitur matrimonium quia existimatur dissolubile . . . non vitiabit contractum . . . Haec autem voluntas generalis debet esse actualis . . . Si autem desit illa voluntas generalis et efficax, tunc secunda voluntas limitat contractum ad matrimonium dissolubile . . . quod eo ipso est invalidum." [81]

In the seventeenth century, following the same authorities, commentators were still divided in their approach to this problem. Thus, upholding the opinion that both parties had to agree to the condition for the invalidating of the contract were such authors as Fa-

---

[79] *Institutiones*, Lib. II, Tit. X, n. 14.
[80] Canon 1084.
[81] *De Sacramentis in Genere*, Disp. VIII, Sec. VIII, nn. 131, 132, 136, pp. 403-404.

gnanus,[82] Pirhing [83] and Laymann.[84]

Basil Pontius (1569-1629), however, writing in the same period, was of the opposite opinion. In his teaching he contended against the eminent authors whose opinion represented the commonly accepted doctrine. He declared that there was no valid marriage, even though only one of the contracting parties injected a condition against indissolubility. This solution he proposed as the only true explanation of the doctrine; to the opposite opinion he denied even the semblance of probability. This was so, he contended, because the bond of marriage resulted from mutual consent and a consent based on a condition contrary to the substance of matrimony is not the consent required for the bond of marriage.[85]

Pontius did not imply that a mere error regarding the nature of the sacrament would invalidate the contract. When he treated of the intention required in the making of the valid contract of marriage he contended that a Catholic must intend what Christ willed by the institution of this sacrament; a heretic must have the intention of doing what Christ ordained or what the true Church teaches, whatever that Church may be.[86] Therefore, even if the error touched

[82] *Commentaria*, Lib. IV, n. 3, p. 42.

[83] *Ius Canonicum*, Lib. IV, Tit. V, § III, XIII, note i, p. 65; cf. also § XIV, note 2, p. 65.

[84] *Theologia Moralis*, Lib. V, Tract. X, Pt. II, Cap. VII, Corr. I, p. 479.

[85] "... vinculum matrimonii claudicare non potest, sed resultat ex consensu duorum mutuo necessario ad matrimonium; at consensus eius qui consentit sub conditione contraria substantiae matrimonii, non est is qui ad coniugium requiritur. Ergo, ex illo et altero pure contrahente non potest oriri vinculum matrimonii. Quod non tantum verum est in foro conscientiae, sed etiam in foro externo, dum constaret de conditione posita ab uno contra substantiam matrimonii."—*Tractatus de Sacramento Matrimonii* (Venetiis, 1756), Lib. III, Cap. XII, n. 8, p. 95.

[86] "Et quidem coniugis Catholici ea intentio esse debet, ut faciat quod Christi institutio voluit, ea enim necessaria est, ut matrimonium sit sacramentum. In heretico quoque sufficit intentio faciendi quod Christus ordinavit, vel vera Ecclesia tenet, quaevis illa sit. Hanc enim intentionem sufficientem esse ad valorem sacramenti . . . quamvis hereticus in particulari errat, existimans suam ecclesiam esse veram, vel Christum nihil instituisse de sacramento matrimonii. Sunt enim isti errores tantum concomitantes matrimonium, nullam vero in illud efficacitatem habent et ideo ex illis nihil vitii in matrimonium derivatum." — *Op. cit., Appendix: De Matrimonio Catholici Cum Heretico*, Cap. IX, n. 9, p. 540.

the essential note of indissolubility, it did not, if it was truly a concomitant error only, invalidate the contract. One had expressly, whether externally or internally, to intend to contract a dissoluble union before the contract for marriage became vitiated and invalid.[87]

3. The Effect of Subsequent Intercourse on the Conditional Consent

For the status of the marital union Sanchez held that it made no difference whether or not an act of carnal intercourse had followed after the attaching of a condition against the substance of marriage in the marriage contract; in either case the contract was and remained void.[88] This opinion had been accepted by Covarruvias as the common opinion.[89]

Much of the difficulty in this question derived from the decretal *Per tuas nobis* of Pope Innocent III.[90] Commenting on this passage, Soto limited this presumption for the validity of the marriage to the external forum, not extending it to the forum of conscience, even

[87] "Quamvis hereticus eum errorem habeat et mente retineat vel explicet, si tamen vult contractum matrimonii celebrare iuxta suam naturam, quaecumque illa sit, valebit contractus et erit insolubilis, quia error ille tantum est concomitans et ab eo nullum vitium in matrimonium derivatur . . . Si vero expresse velit ita contrahere et non aliter, sive eum animum explicet, sive mente retineat, nullum est matrimonium. Est enim ea matrimonii qualitas, cui innititur is contrahens, veluti quaedam conditio, quae est contra substantiam matrimonii et conditiones contra substantiam vitiant matrimonium." — *ibid.*, n. 11, p. 541.

[88] Cf. Sanchez, *De Matrimonii Sacramento*, Lib. V, Disp. XIII, n. 4, p. 317.

[89] "Nihil referre an copula subsequatur, quando matrimonium fuit contractum, adiecta ex utriusque consensu conditione contra substantiam actus; ille enim contractus nullus est, nec valet in vim sponsalium; igitur coitus efficere nequit matrimonii praesumptionem, secundum communem opinionem."—*De Matrimonio*, Pars II, Cap. III, § 1, n. 17, p. 183.

[90] This seem irrelevant when one considers the background of this decretal. The case there proposed was one in which the condition depended on a third person, other than the parties to the contract, as is expressed in the condition itself "*si pater tuus consenserit.*" Our problem refers to a condition attached by the parties to the contract themselves.

when a carnal intercourse had followed; in the forum of conscience it was not an act of conjugal intercourse, but fornication.[91]

Barbosa (1589-1649) appealed to the Tridentine legislation as expressed in the decree *Tametsi*[92] in holding that a union, when contracted under a condition against the very substance of marriage, could not ultimately eventuate as a valid marital union in view of the ensuing act of carnal intercourse.[93] This assertion was later supported by Pirhing who likewise contended that the decree *Tametsi* nullified the opinion which regarded the subsequent act of intercourse as ratifying the previous qualified consent.[94]

Pontius did not leave room for any distinction between the pre- and post-Tridentine law on this point. He did not agree that validity for such a marriage could have arisen before the Council of Trent (with the union honored as valid in those places where the decree *Tametsi* had not yet been promulgated) and that invalidity was its continuing lot only after the doctrine of the Council of Trent had been received. A union so contracted was and remained invalid before as well as after the Council of Trent for the same reason:

> "Quia matrimonium illud fuit a principio nullum. Ergo, copula postea secuta non efficitur validum . . . Non est unde praesumitur consensus matrimonii in hoc casu."[95]

This invalidity he related exclusively to the case wherein the condition was attached as a resolvent condition by one of the parties. If the attached condition was of a suspensive character, then a valid union could set in with the verification of the invoked condition.

---

[91] "Intelligitur autem matrimonium esse tunc praesumptum in foro ecclesiae: nam in foro conscientiae, si quis sub conditione contraxerat, non accedit affectu maritali sed fornicario, non discedit a conditione, nec perfecit matrimonium."— *Commentarium*, Vol. II, Dist. 29, Q. II, Art. III, pp. 190-191.

[92] *Canones et Decreta C. Tridentini, Decretum*, Sess. XXIV, Cap. 1, De Reform., pp. 216-218.

[93] "Etiamsi post matrimonium sub conditione vel modo illo contractum sequeretur carnalis copula, non efficeret ut matrimonium omnino nullum, propter prolem supervenientem revivisceret. Quae quidem opinio hodie sine dubio procedit cum per Concilium Tridentinum subsequens copula nihil efficiat." — *Collectanea*, Vol. II, Tit. V, n. 7, p. 45.

[94] *Jus Canonicum*, Lib. IV, Tit. V, § II, VI, note 2, p. 64.

[95] *Tractatus de Sacramento Matrimonii*, Lib. III, Cap. XII, nn. 10-11, p. 95.

The invoking of a suspensive condition did not militate against the sacramental substance, *"sed [esset] tantum turpe, et ideo reiici et circumscribi."* Under these circumstances, *"matrimonium erit ab initio purum, et secuta copula etiam id ostendet."* [96]

D. MAJOR CLARIFICATIONS OF THE DOCTRINE IN THE 18TH CENTURY

1. DOCTRINE ON THE TYPES OF CONDITIONS

The doctrine of Sanchez, in most of the important matters under discussion in the previous centuries, had by the 18th century become common doctrine. Prospective conditions *(de futuro)* against the substance of marriage rendered the contract invalid, since the contract evinced a lack of consent. A resolvent condition, the effect of which would have been the rescinding of the marriage contract on the later verification of the invoked condition, could not be employed in a contract of marriage, for marriage is indissoluble by its very nature. Even an invoked impossible condition could entail invalidity for the marriage contract if it was seriously invoked against the substance of marriage. Although in the forum of conscience one had to pay heed to the real intention of either one of the parties, regardless of what kind of condition was invoked, as long as it was seriously entertained, nevertheless in the external forum one had to stand by the dispositions of law. For this reason those who contracted marriage were presumed to do so according to the mind of the Church. This presumption stood until it was disproved. As supporting this doctrine one may name the various important figures of the eighteenth century. [97]

[96] Pontius, *loc. cit.*

[97] Cf. La Croix (1652-1714), *Theologia Moralis* (Coloniae, 1719), Vol. II, Lib. VI, *De Sacramentis*, Pars III, Tract. VI, Cap. II, D. I, n. 223, p. 450; also *ibid.*, n. 239, § 1, p. 453; Schmaltzgrueber (1663-1735), *Ius Ecclesiasticum*, Lib. IV, Tit. V, n. 115, pp. 435-436; F. Schmier (1680-1728), *Jurisprudentia Canonico-Civilis, seu Ius Canonicum Universum* (2 vols., Venetiis, 1754), Vol. II, Lib. IV, Tr. II, Cap. II, Sec. III, § 1, nn. 97-98, 109-112, p. 395 (hereafter cited *Jurisprudentia*); Pichler (1670-1736), *Ius Canonicum secundum V Decretalium Titulos Explicatum* (2 vols., Revennae, 1741), Vol. I, Lib. IV, Tit. V, n. 12, p. 541; Maschat (1692-1747), *Institutiones Canonicae* (Romae, 1757), Pars. II, Lib. IV, Tit. V, nn. 17-20, pp. 349-351; Amort (1692-1747), *Elementa Iuris Canonici Veteris et Moderni*, Vol. II, *Ius Canonicum Modernum* (Ferrariae, 1763), Lib. IV, Tit. V, § 3-5, pp. 384-385; Devoti (1744-1820), *Institutiones Canonicae* (4. ed., 4 vols., Venetiis, 1827), Vol. II, Lib. II, Tit. II, Sec. IX, § 146, p. 220.

2. DOCTRINE ON THE *Deductio in Pactum*

Discussion still continued in the eighteenth century on the question of whether both parties had to agree on the condition if it was to have an invalidating effect, or whether the invoking of the condition by one alone could suffice to render the contract null. Among the authorities supporting the view that both had to agree on the condition one finds Schmalzgrueber,[98] and Maschat;[99] on the other hand, authors like La Croix [100] and Pichler [101] held that *"si solum unius intentio sit nulla, totum sacramentum est nullum."* [102]

In the 18th century, because of the two definite declarations of the Congregation of the Holy Office at the end of the previous century,[103] in which the answers to questions proposed regarding the validity of marriages of apostates from the faith contained the declaration: *"si adsit pactum dissolubilitatis, non esse matrimonium neque sacramentum; si vero non adsit, esse matrimonium et sacramentum,"* [104] and: *"si ista sint deducta in pactum, seu cum ista conditione sint contracta, matrimonia sunt nulla,"* [105] one finds a clear teaching on the nature of the *"deductio in pactum."* The problem of the validity of marriages among the dissidents who taught the dissolubility of marriage for adultery and other causes occupied a great deal of attention in this period. Authors found great value in the teaching of De Lugo, distinguishing a condition against sacramental perpetuity from a merely speculative error concerning indissolubility. Because of this distinction, De Lugo's principle was that the general intention of doing what Christ instituted pre-

---

[98] *Ius Ecclesiasticum*, Lib. IV, Tit. V, nn. 116-117, p. 436.

[99] *Institutiones Canonicae*, Pars II, Lib. IV, Tit. V, n. 17, p. 350.

[100] *Theologia Moralis*, Vol. II, Lib. VI, Pars III, Tr. VI, Cap. II, D. I, n. 254, p. 457.

[101] *Ius Canonicum*, Vol. I, Lib. IV, Tit. V, n. 12, p. 541.

[102] La Croix, *loc. cit.*

[103] S.C.S. Off. (Basniae), 2 dec. 1680, and S.C.S. Off. (Mission. Capuccin.), 23 iul. 1698 — *Codicis Iuris Canonici Fontes, cura Eͫi. Petri Card. Gasparri editi* (9 vols., Romae [postea Civitate Vaticana], Typis Polyglottis Vaticanis, 1923-1939 [Vols. VII-IX, *ed. cura et studio Eͫi. Iustiniani Card. Serédi*]), nn. 755: 761 (hereafter cited *Fontes*).

[104] *Fontes*, n. 761.

[105] *Fontes*, n. 755.

vails over the merely concomitant error that marriage is dissoluble
for a cause, unless it is overthrown by a particular intention contrary to indissolubility. This principle was now generally accepted
and was embodied in a decision of the Sacred Congregation of the
Council.[106]

This teaching was incorporated into the work *"De Synodo Diocesana"* by Prosper Lambertini (1675-1758), who ruled as Pope
Benedict XIV from 1740 to his death. Many of the decisions of the
Sacred Roman Rota and of the Sacred Congregations quoted his
doctrine as the basis for an interpretation on matters regarding validity in marriages, especially the marriages of heretics and infidels.
This doctrine was essentially the same as that of De Lugo: simple
error about the perpetual nature of marriage did not invalidate a
marriage, as long as it was not incorporated into the contract as a
condition thereof; the general intention of entering a marital contract as Christ had instituted it absorbed, as it were, the private
error that marriage was dissoluble in a case of adultery. Where,
however, the parties added an express intention of dissolving the
marriage in case of adultery, this general intention would be ex-
tinguished by such a particular intention.[107]

[106] *Thesaurus Resolutionum Sacrae Congregationis Concilii* (167 vols., Urbino:
vols. I-V, 1739-1740: Romae: vols. VI ff. 1741-1908). Vol. V (1745). Proceedings of Sat., 9 feb. 1732, pp. 261-262 (hereafter cited *Thesaurus*).

[107] "Validum firmumque haberi debeat matrimonium eorum, qui nulla apposita
conditione huiusmodi, alteri nubent, etiamsi falsam illam opinionem foveant, qua
putent, matrimonium ipsum, fracta per adulterium fide, solutum iri; contra vero
nullum et irritum censendum sit matrimonium eorum, qui praeter eum errorem,
quo imbuti sint, conventionem etiam adiiciunt de matrimonii dissolutione quoad
vinculum, interveniente adulterio. Super quo ita rationantur: quicumque contractum vult, necesse est, ut eiusdem substantiam velit; ideoque, si contrahentes, in
matrimonii foedere ineundo, conditionem apponunt illius substantiae contrariam,
certissimum hoc est argumentum, nequaquam eos in veri matrimonii contractum
consentire; sine contrahentium autem consensu, matrimonium esse non potest.
Quod si expressa illa conditio . . . apposita minime fuerit, quantumvis contrahentes in eo fuerint errore, . . . locus est praesumptioni, ut dum matrimonium,
prout a Christo institutum fuit, inire voluerunt, illud omnino perpetuum, ac, interveniente etiam adulterio, insolubile contrahere voluerint; praevalente nimirum
generali, quam diximus, voluntate de matrimonio iuxta Christi institutione ineundo, atque privatum illum errorem quodammodo absorbente, quo fit, ut matrimonium ita contractum, validum firmumque maneat.

Basing his doctrine on decisions in two cases which occured in Transylvania, in which marriages with conditions against indissolubility were declared null, Benedict taught that the expression *"in pactum deductum"* signified a true condition, attached by one or both parties, which affects the validity of the matrimonial consent and contract.[108]

3. DOCTRINE ON THE EFFECT OF SUBSEQUENT INTERCOURSE

The doubt relating to this question was laid to rest in the 18th century. The settling of the doubt derived mainly from a decision of the Sacred Congregation of the Council in the case of a marriage contracted in Lisbon on 6 May, 1718, in which, after a conditional consent, a man was said to have withdrawn his condition because he had conjugal relations with the woman in question. The Council declared: *"Recessus a protestatione per copulam subsecutam procedere de jure canonum, secus autem de jure conciliari"* and declared the marriage in question null.[109] In addition to this decision there was another by the same Sacred Congregation regarding a marriage which took place at Eichstaedt, in Bavaria, *"ad quam provinciam Tridentinis legibus nunquam patuit additus"*. In this union the conjugal relations had to be taken into account for the reaching of a decision whether a party had withdrawn a suspensive condition.[110]

"At, ubi contrahentes in ipso matrimonii contractu expressam apposuerunt conditionem de dissolvendo quoad vinculum matrimonii in casu adulterii; iam fieri nequit, ut error particularis absorptus maneat a generali voluntate contrahendi matrimonium, prout a Christo Domino institutum fuit: sed potius voluntas generalis eiusmodi extinguitur et suffocatur ab errore particulari, qui manifeste praevalet ac dominatur; atqui hinc oritur nullitas matrimonii, in quo contrahendo apposita fuit conditio ipsius substantiae contraria."—Benedictus XIV, *De Synodo Diocesana* (4 vols., Romae, 1783), Vol. III, Lib. XIII, Cap. XXII, n. VII. pp. 293-294.

[108] "Irrita et nulla esse connubia in quibus id expresse consultum fuerit tamquam pactum atque conditio."—*Op. cit., ibid.*, nn. VIII-IX, pp. 294-295.

[109] *Canones et Decreta C. Tridentini*, Sess. XXIV, *Declarationes et Resolutiones*, n. 88, Response of S. C. of Council of July 8, 1724, p. 250; S.C.C., Ulixbonen., 8 iul. 1724—*Fontes*, n. 3278.

[110] *Thesaurus*, Vol. V (1745), Proceedings of Saturday, 9 Feb. 1732, pp. 258-261.

From a consideration of these two decisions, it seems that the Sacred Congregation favored the opinion of Barbosa and Pirhing, which, with regard to the validity of such a marriage, distinguished between the areas where the decree *Tametsi* had or had not been promulgated. In the case arising in Lisbon, where the decree *Tametsi* had been promulgated, the subsequent act of intercourse had no effect on the invoked condition, and thus the marriage was regarded as invalid. In the case occuring in Bavaria, where the Tridentine decree had not been promulgated, the subsequent carnal intercourse had to be considered as a factor regarding the withdrawing of the invoked condition.

With the passing of the 18th century, however, this matter of subsequent intercourse as a validating factor became a matter of academic interest only. It was not to be an important consideration in later canonical commentary.

A fixed doctrine regarding the invalidity of a marriage contract to which was attached a condition contrary to the indissolubility of the marriage bond was thus essentially established by the beginning of the nineteenth century. For this reason the canonical commentary of the authors, together with the instructions and decisions of the Sacred Congregations, can from that period forward be classified as modern commentary, and it will be utilized as such in this dissertation.

PART II
CANONICAL COMMENTARY

CHAPTER III
PRELIMINARY NOTIONS

Article I. Marriage — Its Definition and Nature

Before and after the Church of Christ, the institute of marriage existed and still continues to exist as an institution of the natural law, as that institution which God, the Author of nature, established in the Garden of Eden as a suited and apt means for the conservation of the human race. Inasmuch as marriage had lost this primal dignity, impressed on it by the very Author of nature, Christ, the Restorer of all things, reclaimed for its former dignity and nobility for all men. Furthermore, for the baptized He enhanced that dignity with the added nobility of supernatural grace by elevating marriage to the high estate of a sacrament.[1]

The institute of marriage can be considered in an active sense (*"in fieri"*) or in a passive sense (*"in facto esse"*). Marriage, when one considers it as a contract and abstracts altogether from the notion of a sacrament, can be defined as a contract by which a man and a woman mutually grant and accept the right over the body of the other, which right is perpetual and exclusive, with a view to the exercise of acts which are essentially fitted for the procreation of offspring.[2] This matrimonial contract is called matrimony *"in fieri"*; the conjugal union which results from this contract is called matrimony *"in facto esse"*.[3] If, however, one considers matrimony as a sacrament, in its metaphysical essence, then, in company with most of the authors, one may define it as a *"coniunctio maritalis, spiritualis gratiae collativa"* or a *"contractus marem et feminam, nullo iure impeditos, ad individuam vitae societatem, et corporum ad actus coniugales traditionem mutuam obligans, iisque rite dispositis conferens gratiam sanctificantem."*[4] This must be noted in

---

[1] Canon 1012, § 1. Cf. Vlaming, *Praelectiones Iuris Matrimonii* (4. ed., a L. Bender, O.P., Bussum in Hollandia: Paulus Brand, 1950), p. 2.

[2] "Matrimonium, quatenus est contractus, in se spectatus, seu abstractione facta a ratione sacramenti, definiri potest: 'contractus quo vir et mulier sibi mutuo tradunt et acceptant ius in corpus, perpetuum et exclusivum, in ordine ad actus per se aptos ad generationem'." — De Smet, *De Sponsalibus et Matrimonio*, n. 75, pp. 58-59.

[3] De Smet, *ibid.*, cf. note (1) to n. 76, p. 59.

[4] Cf. Schmalzgrueber, *Ius Ecclesiasticum*, Lib. IV, Tit. 1, n. 288.

the two aspects of the contract, namely, that the nature of the contract as a natural institution was not changed in any way through its elevation to the sacramental dignity.[5] Rather, the unaltered contract between baptized persons is itself the sacrament of matrimony, as is evident from the disposition of canon 1012, § 1: *"Christus Dominus ad sacramenti dignitatem evexit ipsum contractum matrimonialem inter baptizatos."* These definitions of matrimony *"in fieri"* and *in facto esse"* are commonly accepted by the authors.[6] In this study the interest centers on the contract itself, the *"matrimonium in fieri"*, since an invalidating condition can be attached to the contract only in its making; such a condition can not affect a valid contract already made.[7]

Marriage is, then, by definition, a bilateral contract between a man and a woman in a true and proper sense of the term "contract", as is evident from a simple analysis of the notion of contract as applied to marriage. For a true bilateral contract is nothing else than the legitimate consent given to the same thing by two or more persons who are free to act in law, which consent induces an obligation that binds the parties in commutative justice to give or to withhold something, or to do something or leave it undone. The various elements relating to a contract are therefore: some action on the part of two or more persons, a legal freedom for them to act, an agreed object, a mutual obligation binding in commutative justice and the consent of the parties to the contract. Among all people these elements are found in the marriage contract, for marriage is effected by means of the true, legitimate consent of a man and a woman, who are free to act, and through that act grant to each other the true and mutual right over their bodies for the generation and education of children.[8]

---

[5] Capello, *Summa Iuris Canonici*, Vol. II (4. ed., Romae, 1945), n. 295, p. 285 (hereafter cited as *Summa*).

[6] Cf. Cappello, *loc. cit.;* Coronata, *De Matrimonio*, n. 2, p. 2; Sanchez, *De Matrimonii Sacramento*, Lib. II, Disp. 1, n. 1.

[7] For a treatment of the disputed question whether the notion of the sacrament fits only the *"matrimonium in fieri"* or also the *"matrimonium in facto esse"*: cf. Coronata, *De Matrimonio*, Tit. VII, Art. I, n. 2, p. 2 and n. 14, p. 17.

[8] Cf. Wernz-Vidal, *Ius Matrimoniale*, n. 34, pp. 42-43.

At the same time marriage is a bilateral contract which is singular in many respects, a contract which is *"sui generis."* In its origin it is a natural contract, which is based on nature itself and is directed to the good of the whole human race, and not to the good of the parties alone. By reason of the quality of the consent given, it supersedes every other natural contract, since this consent cannot be supplied by any other human power, nor can the rights which are derived from this consent be transferred, as can be done by sale, prescription, etc., in other contracts. The marriage contract differs from other contracts by reason also of its principal object; in other contracts, many of the conditions, obligations and effects can be determined by the private will of the parties, and the terms of the contract can be changed by the same will. In marriage, however, all the elements which are substantial to the contract are determined in their nature, and the will of the parties does not lend any determination to them. Finally, the marriage contract is of a preeminent character by reason of its firmness and duration, for in other contracts the parties have the right to break the contract by mutual agreement or by other lawful means. In marriage, however, the wills of the contracting parties are so bound that they can never rescind the contract by mutual consent, once that contract has been made validly. From this it follows that, even apart from its elevation to the status of a sacrament, the marriage contract is never a merely civil, profane contract, but is, by nature, something holy and religious.[9]

There are authors who, because of these specific differences between the matrimonial contract and other contracts, dislike the usage of the term "contract" in respect to it. This objection has little basis. Marriage can be called a contract with full right, since the *"consensus duorum in idem placitum"*, the constitutive note of a contract, is found in the consent of a man and a woman to a mutual conjugal life, and since *"contractus denominatio, matri-*

---

[9] Cf. Wernz-Vidal, *Ius Matrimoniale*, n. 35, pp. 44-45; Coronata, *De Matrimonio*, Art. I, § 2, p. 2.

*monio applicata, passim invenitur non solum apud optimae notae
theologos et canonistas, sed in ipsis iuris ecclesiastici fontibus."*[10]
Therefore, the use of the term "contract" is not unbefitting to the
nature of matrimony, nor does the term imply an incorrect concept.
Thus the Code uses the term in reference to marriage,[11] as does the
encyclical letter *Casti connubii* of Pope Pius XI.[12] Thus, depite individual divergencies between it and other contracts, matrimony
also has the true nature of a contract.[13] Yet, it must be stressed that
even among infidels the marriage contract is not a mere civil contract, for as Pope Leo XIII has pointed out: *"inest in eo sacrum et
religiosum quiddam, non adventitium, sed ingenitum, non ab hominibus acceptum, sed natura insitum."*[14] In the same way, Sipos
(1875-1949), repeating the words of Pope Leo, stated that *"sua vi,
sua natura, sua sponte est res sacra, a Deo ordinata."*[15] Because of
this sacred nature, there are attributed to the matrimonial contract
certain unique characteristics, which both intrinsically and extrinsically differentiate the nuptial contract from other contracts. Intrinsically, the marriage contract has this unique note that the consent of the parties to it cannot be supplied by any human law,
whereas in many cases human laws can supply for defect of consent
in other contracts. Extrinsically, the marriage contract has, by divine
law, two unique elements in that God, from the beginning, added
two conditions to the marriage contract which do not depend in

[10] Vlaming, *Praelectiones Iuris Matrimonii*, Part. I, Chap. II, pp. 2-3.

[11] Cf. canon 1012, § 1.

[12] Cf. Pius XI, litt. encycl. *Casti connubii*, 31 dec. 1930—*Acta Apostolicae Sedis,
Commentarium Officiale* (Romae, 1909-   ), XXII (1930), p. 549 (hereafter
cited *AAS*).

[13] Cf. Sipos, *Enchiridion Iuris Canonici*, § 96, p. 405; Vlaming, *loc. cit.* There
are others who deny that marriage is a contract at all. For a rebuttal of these,
cf. Vlaming, *Praelectiones Iuris Matrimonii*, pp. 3-4.

[14] Leo XIII, ep. encycl., *Arcanum*, 10 febr. 1880—*Acta Sanctae Sedis, In Compendium Opportune Redacta et Illustrata, studio et cura Josephi Pennacchi et
Victorii Piazzesi* (41 vols., Romae, Typis Polyglottae Officinae S.C. De Propoganda Fide, 1865-1908), XII (1878-1880), 392 (hereafter cited *ASS*).

[15] Sipos, *Enchiridion Iuris Canonici*, § 96, p. 405.

any way on the will of the parties to that contract. These characteristics are unity and indissolubility.[16]

These qualities of unity and perpetuity are called essential properties of marriage, because they automatically and necessarily flow from the nature of marriage itself, so that without these qualities marriage neither can exist nor can it be mentally conceived as existing.[17] By reason of the sacramental character inherent in a Christian marriage these qualities obtain a special firmness,[18] for marriage, as a sacrament, signifies the union of Christ and His Church and thus is more perfect by far than the marriage of infifels.[19] The quality of indissolubility is necessary to marriage by its nature since the opposite is inimical to the nature of the conjugal union, in that it destroys the equality of the partners; it undermines the mutual duties of the parties; it inflames rather than serves as a remedy against concupiscence, and it endangers the procreation and education of children, the good of the family and of the whole human race.[20]

[16] "Interponitur discrimen inter contractus reliquos et contractum connubialem. Quod quidem duplex est, alterum intrinsecum, extrinsecum alterum. Intrinsecum illud est quod oritur ex ipsa rei natura, quatenus consensus ex parte contrahentium coniugum sic debeat liber esse, ut huic defectui nulla humana lex supplere possit, secus ac respectu ceterorum contractuum pluribus in casibus contingat. Extrinsecum vero illud censetur quod provenit ex iure divino positivo, quatenus Deus in ipsa coniugii institutione a mundi primordiis duas apposuerit conditiones contractui matrimonii, quae a nulla humana potestate pendeant, cuiusmodi sunt unitas et indissolubilitas, quas cum Deus ipse iure suo in veteri lege mitigaverit, Christus in nova ad pristinam sanctitatem revocavit."—Gerdilius, *Trattato del Matrimonio* (Romae, 1803), Pars I, § 1, pp. 32-34 as cited in Perrone, *De Matrimonio Christiano* (3 vols., Romae, 1858), Vol. II, Chap. I, Art. III, p. 31.

[17] "Unitas et indissolubilitas dicuntur proprietates essentiales matrimonii, quia sponte ac necessario ita profluunt ex ipsa coniugii natura ut sine iisdem matrimonium nec subsistere neque concipi possit." — Cappello, *Summa*, II, n. 298, p. 287.

[18] Canon 1013, § 2.

[19] "Dicuntur in matrimonio Christiano peculiarem obtinere firmitatem ratione sacramenti, quia matrimonium, prout est sacramentum, longe perfectius quam infidelium coniugium unionem Christi cum Ecclesia significat."—Cappello, *loc. cit.*

[20] "Dissolutio adversatur paritati viri et mulieris in matrimonio, mutuo obsequio sibi a coniugibus in rebus domesticis impendendo; non sopit, imo inflammat concupiscentiam, periclitat procreationem et educationem prolis, bonum status et generis humani."—Sipos, *Enchiridion Iuris Canonici*, § 96, 5, p. 406.

Indissolubility of a marriage contract carries this import, that the bond of marriage by which a man and a woman are united in marriage, and which is produced by the contract of matrimony, must be perpetual, so that, as long as both parties live, that bond cannot end. This indissolubility can be intrinsic or extrinsic. Intrinsic indissolubility is that by which the marriage bond cannot be dissolved by the mutual consent of the partners nor by its nature; extrinsic indissolubility is that by which it is not dissolved by the intervention of any public authority.[21] In this dissertation, the interest centers upon intrinsic indissolubility. By both the natural and the positive divine law, every valid marriage when once contracted, even by infidels, partakes of this internal indissolubility, so that it can never be dissolved by the consent of the parties nor by its nature.[22]

Thus, although the essence of marriage consists in this mutual consent of the parties to the giving and accepting of the rights over the bodies of each other, so that the Code holds expressly that *"matrimonium facit partium consensus,"*[23] nevertheless the marriage bond was established by God with these peculiar qualities. What God has joined together, man cannot put asunder. The parties can will or decline to enter upon such a contract of marriage, as they freely choose, but once this contract has been concluded and a valid

---

[21] Cf. Coronata, *De Matrimonio*, Art. I, § 10, p. 11. Coronata, quoting Vlaming (*Praelectiones*, n. 18), indicates that both unity and indissolubility are included in the designation of the *"individua vitae consuetudo"* recognized as the essence of marriage in Roman Law . . . *"non enim intelligitur inter virum et mulierem societas vitae quae vere sit individua, si in eam, stante matrimonio, aut alii admittantur aut post aliquod spatium transactum societas dissolvatur."* He notes, however, that *"indissolubilitatem tamen ius romanum, ut notum est, non admisit."* —Coronata, *op. cit.*, note 4, § 7, p. 8.

[22] "Quodcumque matrimonium valide contractum, etiam infidelium, tum iure naturae tum lege positiva divina indissolubilitate intrinseca gaudet, ita ut nullo in casu possit contrahentium consensu aut natura sua dissolvi." — Cappello, *Summa*, II, Cap. VIII, Art. I, n. 300, p. 288.

[23] Canon 1081, § 1.

union has resulted, changing the qualities of this contract is beyond the discretion of the contracting parties.[24]

Since this matrimonial contract must be consented to by the parties, one should indicate here the essential object and elements of a valid union which the parties must know and freely accept. The essential object of the contract, that which the couple intend with their will to enter marriage, is a *"societas permanens inter virum et mulierem ad filios procreandos,"* [25] which community of life is effected by their mutual giving and accepting of those bodily rights which are naturally fitted for the procreation of children.[26] The ends of marriage are primary and secondary. The primary end is the procreation and education of children; the secondary end is the mutual aid afforded by the parties and the remedy for concupiscence that each provides for the other.[27] The procreation of offspring, namely the conception and birth of children resulting from the physical intimacy of man and woman, is the natural effect of the use of the rights of marriage in the marital act of intercourse. The education of the children thus brought into life must comprehend the development of the whole person: the moral and religious, as also the physical and civil, upbringing of the child, as well as the provision to be made for his temporal welfare.[28] The mutual aid referred to is that conjugal partnership by which the parties in that marriage complement each other physically, spiritually and psychologically. The other secondary end, after the fall of our first parents, is the remedy for concupiscence through acts objectively utilized in harmony with the end of marriage and the moderating norm of right reason.[29] Thus, the marriage union af-

---

[24] For a full discussion of whether every matrimonial bond is soluble by divine authority, although insoluble by any human authority, cf. Coronata, *De Matrimonio*, Art. I, § 10, pp. 12-13.

[25] Canon 1082, § 1.

[26] Canon 1081, § 2.

[27] Canon 1013, § 1.

[28] "Parentes gravissima obligatione tenentur prolis educationem tum religiosam et moralem, tum physicum et civilem pro viribus curandi, et etiam temporali eorum bono providendi."—Canon 1113.

[29] Cf. Noldin-Schmitt, *Summa Theologiae Moralis* (27. ed., 3 vols., Ratisbonae, Romae, Neo Eboraci, 1940), Vol. III, *De Sacramentis*, n. 504, p. 511.

fords the parties thereto a legitimate outlet for their natural sexual desire, while reason regulates this desire, and the inherent purpose of marriage restrains any indulgence outside the conjugal partnership.

These ends of marriage, both primary and secondary, are essential to the marriage contract, in that the natural inclination of the sexes tends to attain these objects in the marriage union. They differ only in this aspect, that the primary end can only be attained through this institution, whereas the secondary ends, which are also intended and which have their own proper good, must serve the possibility of the primary, in so far as this depends on the parties to the contract.[30] This does not mean, however, that marriage cannot exist without the actual realization of these ends, primary and secondary, since the implementation of these ends depends upon a valid contract already entered.[31]

Because of these essential elements in the marriage contract, authors after St. Augustine distinguished a threefold blessing in marriage: that of offspring, that of fidelity and that of indissolubility (*bonum prolis, bonum fidei, bonum sacramenti*). The blessing of offspring consists in the aptitude of generating and educating children.[32] The blessing of fidelity is that by which the spouses

---

[30] Cf. Noldin-Schmitt, *loc. cit.* There have been authors who asserted that these secondary ends are not subordinate to, but are independent of, the primary end of marriage. Because this departure in thought and speech furnished occasion for errors and uncertainties, the Holy Office, to avert such consequences, considered the following questions: *"An admitti possit quorundam recentiorum sententia, qui vel negant finem primarium matrimonii esse prolis generationem et educationem, vel docent fines secundarios fini primario non esse essentialiter subordinatos, sed esse aeque principales et independentes?"* The reply of the Holy Office was: *"Negative."* — *Decretum Sancti Officii*, 1 apr. 1944—*AAS*, XXXVI (1944), 103.

[31] There are other ends as well which may be intended accidentally: family honor, peace between families, compatibility, the increase of wealth, business interests, delight in beauty, etc. Cf. Noldin-Schmitt, *loc. cit.* These are not essentially related to the marriage contract, although they may honorably be present; accordingly, they have no further place in this study.

[32] "In prole [attenditur], ut amanter suscipiatur, benigne nutriatur, religiose educetur."—St. Augustine, *De Genesi ad Litteram*, IX, 7—*CSEL*, XXXXVIII, 275-276.

obtain a mutual and exclusive right over the bodies of each other in regard to conjugal rights so that, as long as the marriage bond lasts, neither may, without the guilt of adultery, attempt a new marriage with another or have extra-marital relations with another.[33] The blessing of indissolubility, with which this study is concerned, consists in the firmness and perpetuity of the marriage bond,[34] an indissolubility which attaches to the marriage even of infidels, but which has a greater firmness in the marriage of the faithful by reason of the sacrament of matrimony. The greatest degree of firmness is to be found in the consummated marriage of Christians, because of the more perfect notion of the sacrament or of the sacred significance which is found in such a marriage.[35] One must not confuse the notion of *"sacramentum"* as used in the expression *"bonum sacramenti"* with the theological concept of a sacrament. The marriage contracts of both the faithful and the infidels have this element of sacramentality in the former sense, although in a differing degree of perfection, and therefore the *"bonum sacramenti"* or indissolubility applies to both contracts, with an unequal degree of perfection.[36]

The three blessings: offspring, fidelity and indissolubility, all pertain to the essence of marriage, but they do not all pertain to it in the same way. The obligation and the realization of the *bonum sacramenti* begin at the same time, at the moment of matrimonial

[33] "In fide attenditur ne praeter vinculum coniugale, cum altera vel altero concumbatur." — St. Augustine, *loc. cit.*

[34] "In sacramento attenditur, ut coniugium non separetur, et dimissus aut dimissa nec causa prolis alteri coniungatur." — St. Augustine, *loc. cit.*

[35] "Bonum sacramenti habetur in firmitate et indissolubilitate vinculi, quae vel ipsi matrimonio infidelium competit, sed iis fidelibus ob rationem veri sacramenti est maior, maxima autem indissolubilitas in matrimonio consummato christianorum habetur propter perfectiorem rationem sacramenti seu sacrae significationis in eo agnitam."—Wernz-Vidal, *Ius Matrimoniale*, Cap. I, n. 28, pp. 35-36. Cf. Cappello, *Summa*, II, n. 301, p. 288.

[36] "Quod bonum sacramenti in decreto pro armenis appellatur 'indivisibilitas matrimonii'. Et revera nomine tertii illius boni sacramenti intelligitur vinculum morale matrimonii, quod solvi non potest. At sicut apud fideles et infideles habetur aliquod 'sacramentum' matrimonii, sed diverso gradu perfectionis, ita etiam apud eosdem existit bonum sacramenti seu indivisibilitatis, at dispari perfectione."—Wernz-Vidal, *ibid.*, note (49), p. 36.

consent; the realization of the other two depends on the use of the conjugal rights, which use does not pertain directly to the essence of the marriage contract. This distinction of St. Thomas between *"ius"* and the *"usus iuris"* has been accepted by canonists in general.[37]

The three blessings of marriage are essential to the contract, but with reference to their attainment they reflect important differences. Because the blessings of offspring and fidelity cannot be attained without the use of the marital rights, parties to a marriage contract could intend to give and accept these rights, while at the same time they do not intend to avail themselves of their use. This cannot be true of the blessing of sacramental stability, which is enjoyed at the moment of consent, independently of the use of the marriage rights. Marriage cannot, therefore, exist without being a stable and perpetual union.[38]

It is for this reason that, among the three blessings of marriage, the blessing of indissolubility must be conceded the primary place.[39]

With due consideration given to the nature of the marriage contract, one may now invite attention to the efficient cause of that contract, that by which it is brought into being, the *"consensus partium."*

[37] Cf. St. Thomas, *Summa Theologica*, Pars IIIa, *Supplementum*, q. 49, art. 3.

[38] Cf. Griese, *The Marriage Contract and the Procreation of Offspring*, The Catholic University of America Canon Law Studies, n. 226 (Washington, D.C.: The Catholic University of America Press, 1946), pp. 6-7.

[39] "Tria bona ad essentiam matrimonii pertinent ita ut non valeat matrimonium, si per intentionem excludantur, si matrimonium contrahatur cum intentione se non obligandi ad procreationem prolis, ad fidelitatem, ad indissolubilitatem. Si autem coniuges intentionem habeant non implendi obligationes, tunc: sine prole et sine fide matrimonium consistere potest, non autem sine indissolubilitate, quapropter ex tribus bonis primum locum occupat bonum sacramenti."—Sipos, *Enchiridion Iuris Canonici*, § 96, ad 6, p. 406. Cf. Sanchez, *De Matrimonii Sacramento*, Lib. II, Dist. 29, n. 11, p. 116.

ARTICLE II. MATRIMONIAL CONSENT

A. DEFINITION OF CONSENT

"Matrimonium facit partium consensus inter personas iure habiles legitime manifestatus; qui nulla humana potestate suppleri potest.

"Consensus matrimonialis est actus voluntatis quo utraque pars tradit et acceptat ius in corpus, perpetuum et exclusivum, in ordine ad actus per se aptos ad prolis generationem."[40] Consent in any contract in general is an act of the will, assenting with some other person to some object in all those elements which belong substantially to that object. Now the substantial object of marriage is the conjugal union and specifically, the perpetual and exclusive right over the body of the other in relation to those acts naturally apt for generation. For this reason, the matrimonial consent is that act of the will by which each party gives and accepts this right.[41] Since the will, however, in order to act, requires the illumination of the intellect to indicate the object of the act of the will, the will normally acts upon this operation of the intellect to effect the marriage contract.

B. NATURE OF CONSENT AND ITS ESSENTIAL EXPRESSION

In order that this consent of the will may suffice for effecting the matrimonial contract, it must have those qualities which are required for consent in any natural, bilateral contract. Accordingly it must be true, deliberate, mutual, manifested through some external sign by parties who are competent in law to act. By a true consent is meant an internal consent which agrees with the external expression of it (otherwise the consent will be a simulation). A deliberate consent is one that is given with full advertence and perfect consent of the will. The consent is mutual if it is given by both parties to the contract. A consent is legitimately manifested when it is expressed externally in the manner required by law. Lastly, the

---

[40] Canon 1081, § 1, § 2.

[41] Cf. Gasparri, *Tractatus Canonicus de Matrimonio* (*Editio Nova ad mentem Codicis I. C.*, 2 vols., Typis Polyglottis Vaticani, 1932), II, n. 776 (hereafter cited as *De Matrimonio.*)

parties must not be barred by any hindrance or impediment of law which would nullify their right to make such a contract.[42]

If these qualities of the contractual consent are related to the matrimonial consent, one can see that these same characteristics of the consent must be found in the contract of matrimony. The consent has to be *marital,* i.e. it must be directed to the object of the contract, and thus to the giving and accepting of the rights over the body for those acts which are essentially suited for the generation of children. This consent is implicitly contained in the will of entering a permanent association between a man and a woman for the procreation of children. It is not necessary that the spouses know the nature of carnal intercourse and explicitly intend by their consent to exchange with each other the right to it; it is required indeed but it also suffices that they know that marriage is a permanent and exclusive association for the begetting of offspring, and that they intend to enter such an association.[43]

This marital consent must also be *internal,* since it proceeds from the will. Hence, anyone who fictitiously expresses an external consent, without consenting internally, contracts invalidly. This lack of internal consent must be proved in order to make it stand in the external forum, since the internal consent is always presumed to be in conformity with the words and signs used in the celebration of the marriage contract.[44] The act of consent must also be a fully *deliberate* act which requires that one proceed with sufficient discretion and act with an enlightened and mature judgement.[45]

For the effecting of a matrimonial contract, the consent must also be *mutual,* so that both parties to the marriage consent to it in such a way that the consent of the one party continues when the consent of the other is given. This simultaneity need not be physical, for a moral simultaneity suffices. Such a moral simultaneity obtains when the consent of the second party is actually expressed the while the consent of the first party virtually perseveres.[46]

---

[42] Cf. Noldin-Schmitt, *Summa Theologiae Moralis,* III, nn. 623-627, pp. 631-633.
[43] Cf. De Smet, *De Sponsalibus et Matrimonio,* Disp. 2, Art. I, n. 100, p. 83.
[44] Canon 1086, § 1; Cf. De Smet, *loc. cit.*
[45] Cf. De Smet, *loc. cit.*
[46] Cf. De Smet, *ibid.,* pp. 83-84; Cf. Wernz-Vidal, *op. cit.,* n. 452, p. 586.

This consent can come only *from persons who are free in law* to effect a matrimonial contract; they cannot effect a valid union as long as they are subject to some diriment impediment established by the natural or the positive divine law, or by competent human authority.[47]

Finally, this consent must be *manifested* according to law, when competent authority has by law established a prescribed manner in which the consent is to be manifested. This quality, therefore, presupposes the presence of the parties to the contract, either in person or through proxies, and the observance of the form prescribed by law.[48] In addition to these notes, common to all contractual consent, Coronata adds the quality that the consent must be such as to deal with a present reality, *hic et nunc* giving and receiving the rights of marriage.[49]

Some authors held that the quality of full freedom must also be added to these notes, in that an act of the will which is coerced is by its nature insufficient for a valid matrimonial consent. Gasparri disagreed, with good reason, and pointed out: unless the fear be such as will take away the use of reason completely, the will remains free even under the influence of fear, so that by natural law, apart from some provision of positive law, consent extorted under the influence of fear suffices for a valid matrimonial consent.[50]

This consent, as endowed with these aforesaid qualities, is necessary for the contracting of a valid marriage, since the marriage contract effects the subjection of each party to the power of the other, and for this reason the nature of the contract requires the consent of the parties thereto. This mutual consent, by which obligations in justice arise in the relationship of one to the other, induces the na-

---

[47] Cf. De Smet, *loc. cit.*

[48] Canon 1088, § 1, Cf. De Smet, *loc. cit.;* Wernz-Vidal, *op. cit.*, n. 452, p. 586.

[49] "Consensus debet esse de praesenti, non de futuro; seu debet ferri hic et nunc in traditionem et acceptationem iuris in corpus in ordine ad actus de se aptos ad prolis generationem."—Coronata, *De Matrimonio*, Art. I, § 6, p. 7.

[50] ". . . etiam in metu haberi consensum matrimonialem quia voluntas etiam sub metus influxu semper libera manet, nisi metus rationis usum omnino auferat, ideoque consensum, licet metu extortum, per se sufficere, citra ius positivum, ad validitatem matrimonii; ac proinde tò *liber* omisimus."—*De Matrimonio*, Vol. II, n. 776, p. 7.

ture of a true contract, which cannot exist apart from consent and which takes its beginning from the consent.[51] The internal consent of both parties is necessary, since marriage is a contract; this internal consent must be manifested externally. If it is merely internal there is no contract and no sacrament.[52] Only by such a consent, mutually given, can there arise a marital association with its mutual rights and obligations, which is perpetual and beyond the power of the parties to dissolve. So necessary is this consent that "it cannot be supplied by any human power." In many other human contracts, when they are deficient because of the lack of consent on the part of one or both of the parties, the consent can, because of the common good, be sometimes supplied by the supreme social authority.[53] This power over the consent of the contracting parties can never be extended to the giving of the marital right over one's body, and much less can it be supplied against the will of the parties or independently of their desire to contract a marital union.[54] In this vein Pope Pius VI clearly taught that consent "cannot be supplied by paternal authority or by the supreme authority of the Church or of the State; for it belongs exclusively to the bride and bridegroom to transfer to each other ownership of their bodies and to

[51] "Haec unius in alterum potestas cum huius subiectione erga illum ex natura rei haberi non potest sine consensu eius qui alterius potestate subiicitur; cumque potestas et subiectio sit mutua, etiam ex natura rei debet haberi per utriusque partis consensum. Haec mutua conventio, qua utriusque conceditur ius, utriusque inducitur iustitiae obligatio erga alterum, inducit naturam contractus, qui citra consensum non existit et ex consensu initium et statum capit."—Wernz-Vidal, *Ius Matrimoniale*, Cap. I, n. 451, p. 585.

[52] Cf. Payen, *De Matrimonio in Missionibus ac Potissimum in Sinis Tractatus Practicus et Casus* (2. ed., 3 vols., Zi-ka-wei, 1935-1936), II, n. 1592, p. 3 (hereafter cited *De Matrimonio*).

[53] "In contractibus, qui versantur circa res exteriores . . . potest nonnumquam ob bonum commune a suprema auctoritate sociali consensus contrahentium suppleri."—Wernz-Vidal, *Ius Matrimoniale*, Cap. I, n. 451, p. 586; Gasparri, *De Matrimonio*, II, Cap. IV, n. 775, pp. 5-6; Coronata, *De Matrimonio*, Art. I, § 6, p. 7.

[54] "Talis potestas publicae auctoritatis nullo modo potest pertingere neque ad translationem iuris in proprium corpus, neque multo minus ad efficiendam contra ipsorum voluntatem aut independenter ab ipsa unionem animorum inter duas personas in societate coniugali mutuo et perpetuo obligatas."—Wernz-Vidal, *loc. cit.*

take upon themselves the yoke of marriage." [55] It appears also that God cannot supply the essential consent which is thus necessary for a marriage, for the reason simply that marriage, as based on natural law, postulates an exchange of consent between the contracting parties. [56]

This consent is indeed necessary, but it also suffices in itself to effect the marriage contract, so that nothing else is required beyond this consent. In particular, there is precluded all necessity of the actual use of the marital right in an act of intercourse for completing the essential perfection of the marriage contract. This is today the accepted doctrine; the opposite opinion, the *"copula"* theory was a matter of dispute in the middle ages. The theory was initiated by Hincmar of Rheims (806-882), who held that the marriage was not established simply by the mutual consent of the parties, inasmuch as the *copula carnalis* was also to be deemed essential if marriage in its nature was to be complete. [57] In this he was supported by the School of Bologna, but the School of Paris held that consent alone was necessary to establish the marriage contract and make it indissoluble. This latter doctrine became the common view followed by the authors, namely that consent alone is the efficient cause of the marriage, and that the intercourse subsequent to the consent is in no way essential to the validity of the marriage. [58]

This is the clear statement of Wernz-Vidal on the matter of the sufficiency of internal consent, once it was externally manifested, for establishing the marriage bond as indissoluble:

> Consensum internum, legitime externe manifestatum, esse se solo sufficientem ad efficiendum matrimonium, excluso quolibet alio et in particulari exclusa necessitate copulae, sub fundamento iuris Romani constanter in legislatione ecclesiastica fuit

---

[55] Pius VI, *Epistola ad Episcopum Agriensem* (Agria, Eger, Erlau), die 11 iul., 1789, as quoted in Ayrinhac-Lydon, *Marriage Legislation*, n. 188, p. 192. Cf. Gasparri, *De Matrimonio*, II, Cap. IV, n. 775, pp. 5-6.

[56] Cf. Coronata, *De Matrimonio*, Art. I, § 6, p. 7.

[57] Cf. Epistola XXII, *De Nuptiis Stephani et filiae Regimundi comitis*, MPL, CXXVI, 137.

[58] Cf. Wernz-Vidal, *Ius Matrimoniale*, Cap. I, n. 451, p. 584; De Smet, *De Sponsalibus et Matrimonio*, Disp. II, Art. I, pp. 75-82; Coronata, *De Matrimonio*, Art. I, § 6, p. 8.

propositum. Ius Romanum id aperte sanciebat: *"nuptias non concubitus sed consensus facit,"* etiam absque traductione sponsae. (L. 15, D, *de conditionibus,* 35 1). In responso Nicholai I ad consulta bulgarorum (c. 2, C. XXVII, q. 2) dicitur: *"Sufficiat solus secundum leges eorum consensus, de quorum coniunctionibus agitur. Qui consensus, si in nuptiis solus forte defuerit, cetera etiam cum ipso coitu celebrata frustrantur."* Item c. 14, X, *de sponsalibus et matrimonio,* IV, 1: *"Matrimonium solo consensu contrahitur."* [59]

If one considers the concept of marriage in the natural law, the act of carnal intercourse is not only not essential to the contract, but it rather presupposes a marriage that has already been contracted. Otherwise, if the contract were not presupposed, the act of intercourse could only be considered as an act of fornication.[60]

The object of the consent of the contracting parties is the mutual giving and accepting of the perpetual and exclusive right over the bodies of each other for the acts which are of themselves suited for the generation of offspring. Nevertheless, although there must be this giving of the marital right and the acceptance thereof by each party, it is not necessary that there be two formally distinct acts. One and the same act of giving over these rights virtually contains within itself the acceptance of rights over the body of the other party, and the same act of acceptance virtually contains the giving of the rights to the other.[61] The reason for this is the essential relationship of man and wife, since a man cannot be a husband without a wife, nor can there be a wife without a husband, just as there can be no giving over of the right without a corresponding giving of that right by the other.[62]

---

[59] *Ius Matrimoniale,* Cap. I, n. 455, p. 588.

[60] Cf. Vlaming, *Praelectiones Iuris Matrimonii,* Pars I, Corr. II, p. 7.

[61] "Quamquam vero consensus matrimonialis est actus voluntatis, quo pars tradit alteri eiusmodi ius et ab altera traditum acceptat, tamen non est necessarius duplex actus formaliter distinctus, alius scilicet quo ius alteri tradatur, et alius quo ius ab altera traditum acceptetur; sed unus idemque actus traditionis virtualiter continet acceptationem, et unus idemque actus acceptationis traditionem." — Gasparri, *De Matrimonio,* II, n. 777, p. 8; Cf. Wernz-Vidal, *Ius Matrimoniale,* Cap. I, n. 453, pp. 586-587.

[62] Cf. Wernz-Vidal, *Ius Matrimoniale, loc. cit.*

It is also of little importance that there be an immediate acceptance in point of time; there may be an interval of time between the giving of the rights and their acceptance, as long as the consent of the first party morally continues until the acceptance by the other.[63]

One must also note here that it is not necessary for a valid contract that the parties *explicitly* will all these essential elements of the contract. An implicit act of the will suffices for the inclusion of all matrimonial benefits and blessings within the marriage contract. Thus, if the parties want to enter a valid union, they do, as long as the parties do not exclude, by a positive act of their wills, some essential element of the contract. In a case of such exclusion, of course, the consent will be deficient, and there will be no contract of marriage effected. It will be enough, however, to establish a valid marriage that the parties to the contract intend the contract, taken as a whole, as other people are accustomed to do, without adverting specifically to the various essential elements of that marriage contract.[64]

The consent to the mutual giving and accepting of marital rights over the body for the acts proper to generation is not to be confused with the actual use of these rights. One can give these rights in a perpetual and exclusive union, and yet, for a variety of reasons, not exercise such rights.[65] The marriage can exist without the exercise of rights; it cannot come into existence without the essential consent to the giving and accepting of such perpetual rights.

C. Kinds of Consent

There are four different kinds of consent which may influence a contract, based on one accepted division of voluntary acts. An act

---

[63] Cf. Gasparri, *De Matrimonio*, II, n. 778, p. 9; De Smet, *De Sponsalibus et Matrimonio*, Disp. II, n. 101, pp. 83-84.

[64] Cf. Gasparri, *De Matrimonio*, II, n. 780, p. 10; De Smet, *De Sponsalibus et Matrimonio*, Disp. II, n. 100, p. 83.

[65] "Quae mutua traditio et acceptatio iuris in corpus in ordine ad copulam, nequaquam est confundenda cum usu seu exercitio iuris, quod stante potestate permanente variis modis potest esse ligatum."—Wernz-Vidal, *Ius Matrimoniale*, n. 453, p. 587.

is voluntary when it proceeds from the will, as the effect from its cause, with the previous knowledge of the intellect. A voluntary act may be distinguished as actual, virtual, habitual or interpretative, depending on what influence the act of the will exercises with respect to its effect. In the light of this division of consent, the consent is actual if the consent is given here and now, has its effect on the contract and is adverted to when the contract is made. Consent is virtual, if it was once elicited and still continues to exercise an effect on the contract, even though it is not adverted to in the making of the contract. A habitual consent is one which was once elicited and never retracted, but which does not exercise any effect on the contract when it is made. An interpretative consent is one which never was given, but which, because of some inclination of the will toward the object in question, would have been given if the subject had thought of it.[66]

In applying these distinctions to the matrimonial consent, one may say that an interpretative consent will not suffice to effect a valid contract of marriage. It does not even merit the name of a consent, since it never did exist as a factual thing, but would merely have existed in some hypothesis. An actual consent, as is evident, will certainly suffice to effect the marital contract, but it is not essential that the consent be given as an actual consent. Without any doubt also a virtual consent will be enough to effect a valid contract. The consent would, for example, be only a virtual consent if the contracting parties made all the arrangements for the marriage, filled out the interrogatories, etc., but at the time of the actual ceremony answered distractedly to the requisition of their consent. As regards the efficacy of a habitual consent, the authors are in dispute, some holding that a habitual consent will suffice, since marriage by proxy is valid, even though the party to the contract who is acting through the proxy is asleep at the actual time of the giving and accepting of his consent. Others deny this, feeling that in such a case there is present a virtual consent, and not merely a habitual one. As Cardinal Gasparri pointed out, this dispute had to do mostly with semantics,

---

[66] Cf. Noldin-Schmitt, *Summa Theologiae Moralis*, III, n. 20, pp. 17-18.

since a habitual consent, in the sense in which these authors understood it, differed but little from a virtual one.[67]

The matrimonial contract by which a marital union comes into being, then, is the consent of the parties, giving and accepting the bodily rights for procreation, rights perpetual and exclusive. It remains to consider what might impede the effect of this consent.

Article III. Factors Opposed to Matrimonial Consent

To constitute a matrimonial consent essentially, two elements are required: an intellectual apprehension of the object of the consent, since there can be nothing in the will which was not previously in the intellect, and an act of the will which can be reduced to the act of consent itself. Since this is so, the matrimonial consent can be vitiated under either heading; either because there is some defect in the intellectual apprehension of the object, or because, despite a sufficient intellectual apprehension, the will refuses to consent.[68] A defect in intellectual apprehension may come from a deficiency in the discretion required for a matrimonial consent, or from intellectual error. The factor opposed to matrimonial consent may come from the will in that there may be a refusal to consent or in that there is a simulation of the consent. Consideration will be given to these possibilities, in so far as they may constitute matter for discussion in the present study.

[67] "Contracto autem matrimonio, nomine consensus virtualis seu habitualis intelligitur idem consensus primitivus non revocatus; cum enim pars voluit tradere-acceptare ius coniugale, praeterito actu physico volitionis in eadem voluntate perseverat et haec voluntas permanens dicitur et est consensus virtualis seu habitualis. Exinde apparet consensum actualem, qui matrimonium efficit, et consensum virtualem seu habitualem post matrimonium esse unum eumdemque numero consensum seu indicare unam eamdemque animi dispositionem tradendi-acceptandi ius coniugale; consensu actuali haec animi dispositio enascitur, et foris exprimitur; virtuali seu habituali continuat, intus in mente reposita, donec revocetur; quae revocatio, utpote factum, non praesumitur, sed claris probanda est argumentis."—Gasparri, *De Matrimonio*, II, n. 781, pp. 10-11.

[68] Cf. Coronata, *De Matrimonio*, Tit. VII, Cap. V, n. 435, pp. 579-580; Gasparri, *De Matrimonio*, II, n. 782, pp. 11-12.

A. Defect on the Part of the Intellect

The deficiency in intellectual apprehension may be rooted in insanity, in a deficiency of requisite discretion or in intellectual error. It is evident that there can be no matrimonial consent if both of the parties, or also only one of them, be insane and therefore incapable of a human act.[69] There must be present a sufficient discretion and use of reason for the constituting of a matrimonial consent. For such a consent *"necesse est ut contrahentes saltem non ignorent matrimonium esse societatem permanentem inter virum et mulierem ad filios procreandos."* [70] This means that such discretion or maturity of mind is required that the parties to the contract understand, at least in a confused fashion, the nature and essential properties of marriage, for otherwise their consent could not be directed to the object of the contract.[71] This knowledge postulates the possession of at least a vague notion of the needed cooperation between the spouses for the having of children. It is not necessary that they know explicitly all those things which pertain to the nature and mode of generation.[72] After puberty any assertion of such ignorance of the essence of marriage must, for a due recognition, be substantiated with proof; such ignorance is not to be presumed.[73] Such factors as these have no immediate place in the present study; the third possibility, that of a defective intellectual apprehension based on an erroneous judgement, is more important to us.

Error is a false apprehension or a false judgement about something. It differs from ignorance, which is simply a lack of due knowledge, but does not connote any passing of judgement. In error something further is added to ignorance; in law, however, ignorance and error often produce the same effects.[74] Error is substantial (es-

---

[69] Cf. Sipos, *Enchiridion Iuris Canonici*, § 130, p. 496; Wernz-Vidal, *Ius Matrimoniale*, n. 456, p. 588; Coronata, *De Matrimonio*, nn. 436 ff., pp. 580 ff.

[70] Canon 1082, § 1.

[71] Cf. Sipos, *op. cit.*, § 130, p. 496.

[72] Cf. Sipos, *loc. cit.;* Wernz-Vidal, *Ius Matrimoniale*, n. 457, p. 590; Gasparri, *De Matrimonio*, II, n. 783, p. 12.

[73] Canon 1082, § 2.

[74] "In errore aliquid additur ignorantiae; at in iure ignorantia et error plerumque eosdem pariunt effectus."—Coronata, *De Matrimonio*, n. 446, p. 599; Gasparri, *De Matrimonio*, II, n. 789, p. 17.

sential), if it relates to some essential element of the act, in which case there can be no marriage; it is accidental, if the error is centered on some accidental element. In the latter contingency, the marriage is valid. Error, whether substantial or accidental, is error of law, if the false judgement concerns the existence or the intent of the law, or an error of fact, if the false judgement relates to the existence of some fact. This error is antecedent *("causam dans contractui")* if it affects the contracting party before the marriage and if that party would not have entered the contract had the error in question not affected his judgement. It is an incident or concomitant error if it merely accompanies the judgement, so that the contract would have been entered into even if the error had not been present. An error of fact can relate either to the person with whom one intends to contract marriage or to the quality or status of that person; an error of law may concern the nature of marriage, its essential properties, or its validity.[75]

Regarding these various types of error, the Code specifies which of these will invalidate a marriage contract. In canon 1083 it states the following:

§ 1. Error circa personam invalidum reddit matrimonium.

§ 2. Error circa qualitatem personae, etsi det causam contractui, matrimonium irritat tantum:

1°. Si error qualitatis redundet in errorem personae;

2°. Si persona libera matrimonium contrahat cum persona quam liberam putat, cum contra sit serva, servitute proprie dicta.

For matrimonial consent truly to be present, it is necessary that there be no error regarding the essence of marriage, since consent cannot coexist with such an error which has to do with the very element which constitutes the substance of the act; this error of law regarding the substance of marriage invalidates the marriage contract in consequence of the dictate of the natural law itself.[76]

---

[75] Cf. Coronata, *De Matrimonio,* n. 446, pp. 599-600; Sipos, *Enchiridion Iuris Canonici,* § 130, pp. 497-499; Gasparri, *De Matrimonio,* II, n. 789, p. 17; De Smet, *De Sponsalibus et Matrimonio,* n. 523, p. 461.

[76] "Error iuris circa substantiam matrimonii matrimonium irritat ex iure naturali."—Coronata, *De Matrimonio,* n. 447, pp. 600-601.

A clear distinction must be made between such an error about the essence of marriage and a simple error about its essential properties. In regard to the properties of unity and perpetuity, canon 1084 clearly states:

> Simplex error circa matrimonii unitatem vel indissolubilitatem aut sacramentalem dignitatem, etsi det causam contractui, non vitiat consensum matrimonialem.

The reason for the distinction is this: such an error can co-exist with the knowledge of the principal object of marriage, and it is this latter knowledge that is required but also suffices for the validity of the marriage. An error about an essential property of marriage would be verified if one of the contracting parties thought that the bond of marriage could be dissolved, at least in some circumstances, as infidels commonly hold, and as the Greek schismatics hold, who still contend that there can be a full divorce because of adultery, or as do some ignorant Catholics, who believe that a civil divorce permits a subsequent marriage.[77] A simple error in this regard, however, as the Code indicates, is without invalidating effect. The Code designates such an error as *"simple"*, namely as not exercising any influence on the subsequent act of the will. If it did, either in the form of a mutual pact or by way of an attached condition in the contract, then the marriage contract would indeed be invalid. If some essential property is positively excluded from the consent, then the essence of the contract is also excluded. If, however, there is no such positive act of the will, then the marriage is to be deemed valid, because the general will of contracting marriage as it was

---

[77] Cf. Gasparri, *De Matrimonio*, II, n. 807, pp. 27-28. Here one must keep in mind the relationship between canon 1082 and canon 1084. Canon 1082, which treats of the knowledge required for the matrimonial consent, declares that one must know that marriage is *"societas permanens"* between man and woman. Here the reference is to a knowledge which, as a minimum, embraces the note of permanence, as opposed to the notion of a transient union. Permanence in this sense is not the same as indissolubility. From canon 1084 it is evident that a knowledge of indissolubility is not required. What is required, as Bouscaren says, is "the knowledge that marriage is a more or less stable, permanent arrangement, not a mere transient companionship."—Bouscaren-Ellis, *Canon Law, A Text and Commentary* (2nd revised ed., Milwaukee: Bruce Publishing Co., 1953), p. 555.

instituted by God prevails over the simple error and effectively absorbs it.[78] Sipos explained this quite succinctly, when he said:

"Simplex dicitur error, quousque quis, etsi theoretice erroneas teneat doctrinas de proprietatibus matrimonii, positivo tamen actu voluntatis nullam ex eis excludit. Error simplex terminatur in intellectu, quin in voluntatem influat."[79]

This provision of the Code, as is clearly stated in the canon, obtains even if this was an antecedent error. This means that, if the parties had been asked about these essential properties of the marriage contract before they entered into it, they would positively have excluded them. Certainly, unbelievers and non-Catholics who consider marriage a dissoluble contract would frequently exclude the essential element of perpetuity if they were questioned about it. Since they were not so questioned, however, they did not exclude them, and therefore the marriage will be valid, since the contract is rooted in the object to which the consent has been given and not to the cause that led to the giving of the consent.[80] Likewise the circumstances of what *might* have been done does not change the nature of the error, nor does it exert any special influence on the consent.[81]

In this case it is certain that there is actually a consent for the

[78] "Simplex error non vitiat consensum, quia, si, praeter errorem qui exclusive residet in intellectu, habeatur et actus voluntatis positivus, excludens essentiales matrimonii proprietates, sive per modum pacti, sive per conditionis appositionem, matrimonium ipsum irritum fit . . . exclusa enim essentiali proprietate modo positivo, ipsa rei essentia exclusa remanet. Si vero actus positivus volutatis non ponitur, matrimonium valet quia generalis voluntas contrahendi matrimonium, prout a Deo institutum est, praevalet et errorem absorbet."—Coronata, *De Matrimonio*, n. 453, pp. 608-609.

[79] *Enchiridion Iuris Canonici*, § 130, p. 499; Cf. also: Cappello, *Summa*, II, n. 376, p. 347; Wernz-Vidal, *Ius Matrimoniale*, n. 491, p. 620; Vlaming, *Praelectiones Iuris Matrimonii*, p. 385; De Smet, *De Matrimonio*, nn. 528-529, p. 464.

[80] ". . . si partes aut alterutra pars de illis proprietatibus interrogatae eas positive exclusissent. Equidem infideles at acatholici qui matrimonium dissolubile habent, si de illis proprietatibus interrogati fuissent eas plerumque positive excusissent, matrimonium valet, quia non attenditur quid hypothetice fecissent, sed quid de facto fecerint."—Coronata, *De Matrimonio*, n. 453, pp. 608-609. Cf. also Wernz-Vidal, *Ius Matrimoniale*, n. 492, p. 620.

[81] "Nam haec circumstantia nequaquam mutat naturam erroris nec ei peculiarem influxum tribuit in consensum."—Cappello, *Summa*, n. 376, p. 347.

marriage contract, and therefore the marriage is valid. This is evident from the fact that, despite the restricted and even defective outlook of their intellect, the contracting parties intended to enter a true marriage, as it was instituted by God. They did not actually exclude any essential property of that marriage union, even though they would have done so if they had thought of it. That every marriage is to be considered valid is a presumption of law by canon 1014; whether actually a positive, invalidating act of the will was added to this error of the intellect in particular cases is a question of fact, and this fact is to be determined in each case by competent judgement.[82]

If the contracting party, either by an explicit act of the will or by a true mental condition, excludes an essential property of marriage, that marriage is invalid. In this hypothesis, however, such an explicit exclusion was not made. Therefore, by reason of the favor that marriage enjoys,[83] it must be presumed that the contracting parties approached marriage with this general will of entering a true marriage contract, even in the face of their simple error, until it is proved that this error led to the placing of a true condition against an essential property, or to a positive contrary act of the will. Since a condition or positive act of the will evinces a fact, this fact, as all other facts, is to be proved, not presumed.[84]

It may be objected, in this regard, that wherever the laws or moral standards admit the ready obtaining of true divorce from the bond of marriage, one should rather presume that the contracting parties intend to marry within the liberties granted by these laws or standards. If this were so, it would follow that all the marriages entered into in these places would have to be held invalid, unless a contrary intention of entering a perpetual marriage were proved in par-

---

[82] "Agitur tamen de simplici praesumptione . . . utrum autem errori actus positivus voluntatis in singulis casibus accesserit, quaestio est facti, in singulis casibus a iudice definienda."—Coronata, *De Matrimonio*, n. 453, p. 609.

[83] Canon 1014.

[84] "Porro propter matrimonii favorem praesumitur contrahentem ad matrimonium accessisse illa generali voluntate cum simplici errore iuris, donec conditio proprie dicta probetur, eo vel magis quod ille alter positivus voluntatis actus esset factum, facta autem non praesumuntur, sed probantur."—Gasparri, *De Matrimonio*, II, n. 807, p. 28.

ticular cases. Cardinal Gasparri treated this objection, but he regarded it as not admissible that, generally speaking, people in these regions entered marriage while thinking of the dissolving of that marriage, and even less admissible is the thought that they willed to exclude a marriage contract unless such a dissolution of the marriage bond were possible.[85] This argument is supported in the latest editions of the works of Vlaming (d. 1935)[86] and Chelodi (1880-1922).[87]

A further objection might be derived through the words of canon 104, that, with reference to contracts, one may invoke an action for recision in view of the error that furnished cause for the contract. Wherefore, also in the contract of marriage, if such an error led to the giving of the marriage consent, there should be room for invoking a similar action to rescind the contract. This difficulty is removed by the express stipulation of the Code: "... error locum dare potest actioni rescissoriae *ad normam iuris,*" and, as Sipos pointed out, "dispositio canonis 1084 in favorem matrimonii derogat dispositioni generali canonis 104."[88]

B. Defect on the Part of the Will

The consent of the contracting parties as related to the role of the act of the will may be defective in different ways: it may be defective because of force or fear; it may be so because of a positive refusal of consent; it may be deficient by reason of a condition attached to the contract. It has been seen that the essential element of the contract is the consent of the parties. As with any contract, the marriage contract requires that the matrimonial consent be manifested by words or signs, through which the required internal con-

[85] "Nam etiam in regione ubi admittitur divortium quoad vinculum, praesumptio debet esse quam diximus, tum propter favorem iuris, quo gaudet matrimonium, tum quia supponendum est nupturientes, dum ad nuptias ineundas accedunt, saltem generatim loquendo, ne cogitare quidem de solutione vinculi matrimonii, aut de aliis nuptiis ducendis et multo minus haec ita cogitare et velle, ut secus ipsum matrimonium excluderent."—Gasparri, *ibid.,* note 1.

[86] Cf. *Praelectiones Iuris Matrimonii,* Art. II, p. 385.

[87] Cf. Chelodi, *Ius Canonicum de Matrimonio et de Iudiciis Matrimonialibus* (5. ed., recognita et aucta a Pio Ciprotti, Vicenza: Societa Anonima Tepografica Editrice, 1947), Cap. V, n. 113, p. 137 (hereafter cited *De Matrimonio*).

[88] *Enchiridion Iuris Canonici,* § 130, p. 499.

sent is verified in the external order. Thus, St. Thomas taught: "In matrimony there is a contract between husband and wife. Now in every contract there must be an expression of the words by which men bind themselves mutually to one another. Therefore in matrimony also the consent must be expressed in words." [89]

Concerning this external manifestation of consent, the Code states:

Internus animi consensus semper praesumitur conformis verbis vel signis in celebrando matrimonio adhibitis. At si alterutra vel utraque pars positivo voluntatis actu excludat matrimonium ipsum, aut omne ius ad coniugalem actum, vel essentialem aliquam matrimonii proprietatem, invalide contrahit. [90]

If there is a discrepancy between the internal intention and the external manifestation thereof, there results a case of simulation. Simulation of consent is the external manifestation of consent by one who does not at the same time give internal consent, but who, rather, positively excludes consent, whether such an exclusion be made with the agreement of the other party, or by fraud to the deception of the other party. [91]

One can simulate consent in various ways: by a positive contrary act of the will; by simply adding a condition excluding some essential property of marriage; by an agreement entered into against marriage itself, or, as is more easily done, against one of its essential properties. Any of these is sufficient to establish a simulation properly so called, and any will suffice to nullify the contract. It will be difficult, however, to prove such simulation, the difficulty being greater in proving simulation resulting from a positive contrary act of the will, less when it results from a pact or a condition. [92]

---

[89] St. Thomas, *Summa Theologica*, Pars III, Suppl., q. 45, art. 2. This English version is from the Fathers of the English Dominican Province (22 vols., Burns, Oates and Washbourne, Ltd., 1912-1936), XIX, pp. 115-116.

[90] Canon 1086, § 1, § 2.

[91] "Simulare dicitur consensum qui externa manifestatione consentiens, nullum internum consensum, qui vere consensus est, sed potius positive illum excludit, sive id dolo facit decipiendo alteram partem sive id facit pactione cum altera parte inita eaque consentiente."—Coronata, *De Matrimonio*, n. 455, p. 613.

[92] Cf. Coronata, *loc. cit.*

The reason for this is that the specific, external manifestation of consent is presumed in law to reflect the same kind of consent.[93]

The common division of simulation in the jurisprudence of the Sacred Roman Rota is that of total and partial. Total simulation excludes marriage itself or all rights to the conjugal act; partial simulation excludes some essential property of marriage.[94] Partial simulation can be divided by reason of the object or essential property which is excluded. Thus there can be a partial simulation by reason of the exclusion of the blessing of offspring, of fidelity or of the sacramental indissolubility.[95]

If one considers the precise element of the contract which is excluded from the consent in a case of simulation, one may detect a triple division. As Gasparri explained:

> Sicut enim consensus plenus est intentio contrahendi et sese obligandi et tandem implendi, ita contrahens simulate, dum contrahit . . . vel non habet intentionem contrahendi . . . vel habet intentionem contrahendi, sed non sese obligandi . . . vel tandem habet intentionem contrahendi et sese obligandi, sed non implendi.[96]

In the first case there is simulation in the strictest sense, a total simulation; one excludes the matrimonial contract itself, in no way intending to contract marriage, but contradicting the external manifestation of consent with an absolute, internal dissent. This is simulation *with the intention of not contracting at all.*[97] In the second and third cases there is simulation in the less proper sense, partial simulation. The former is a case in which one has the intention of contracting marriage, but of not obligating oneself to the terms of the contract, excluding any bond arising from the contract; the latter

[93] Canon 1086, § 1.

[94] "Simulatio est totalis si excludatur matrimonium ipsum aut omne ius ad coniugalem actum; partialis est si excludatur essentialis aliqua matrimonii proprietas."—Coronata, *op. cit.*, n. 458, p. 615.

[95] "Simulatio partialis dividitur in varias species pro ratione objecti seu proprietatis essentialis quae excluditur et habemus proinde simulationem ob exclusam bonum prolis, fidei et sacramenti."—Coronata, *op. cit.*, n. 458, p. 615.

[96] Gasparri, *De Matrimonio*, II, n. 814, p. 36.

[97] Cf. Coronata, *loc. cit.;* Gasparri, *loc. cit.;* Wernz-Vidal, *Ius Matrimoniale*, n. 460, p. 593; Chelodi, *De Matrimonio*, n. 115, p. 139.

case is verified when one has the intention both of contracting and of obligating oneself and assuming the rights of marriage, but one intends not to fulfill the obligations thus assumed. These two cases are respectively: simulation *with the intention of not obliging oneself,* and simulation *with the intention of not fulfilling the obligations.*[98]

In cases of total simulation, wherein the person has the intention not to contract marriage at all, the matrimonial contract is null. The reason for this is evident: consent is an act of the will, and if it is not present in the will, the external manifestation cannot supply it.[99] Similarly, one who has the intention of contracting marriage, but excludes some essential property with a positive act of the will, contracts an invalid union. This positive act of the will cannot coexist with the prior intention of contracting marriage, but destroys that prior act of the will.[100] In the case of one who has the intention of contracting a union and of obligating himself by it, but who intends not to fulfill the obligations in the contract, there is a true matrimonial consent and the marriage is valid.[101] The reason for this difference is that the essence of marriage requires only the mutual giving and accepting of the rights and duties; the fulfilling of these obligations is not essential to the contract.[102]

[98] Cf. Coronata, *loc. cit.;* Gasparri, *loc. cit.;* Wernz-Vidal, *loc. cit.;* Chelodi, *loc. cit.*

[99] "... voluntas in casu deest, et non concordat cum sui externa manifestatione."—Coronata, *op. cit.,* n. 458, p. 616.

[100] "Item qui animum quidem habet contrahendi, sed proprietatem aliquam positivo voluntatis actu, non simplici errori intellectuali excludit, invalide contrahit, quia hoc positivo actu destruit priorem animum contrahendi, qui cum hoc consistere nequit." — Coronata, *loc. cit.*

[101] As will be explained fully below, this refers to the blessing of offspring (*bonum prolis*) and the blessing of fidelity (*bonum fidei*), but not to the blessing of indissolubility (*bonum sacramenti*), since in the last named there can be no distinction between the intention of contracting the union and that of fulfilling the obligation from that contract in marriage.

[102] "Qui autem animum habet cum contrahendi tum se obligandi, non habet vero animum adimplendi validum consensum ponit quia adimplementum onerum matrimonialium non pertinet ad essentiam contractus matrimonialis et matrimonium in se perfectum est quando onera et iura mutuo consensu accipiuntur et traduntur."—Coronata, *loc. cit.*

In a case of simulation in which, by a positive act of the will, one or both of the parties exclude marriage itself, or the rights to the conjugal act, or an essential property of marriage, there is no true consent and the marriage is thus invalid.[103] Must this positive act of the will be in the form of an agreement, explained by some as *"in pactum deducta,"* or be added as a necessary condition, a so-called *"conditio sine qua non,"* before invalidity results for the contract?

The expression *"in pactum deducere"* can signify that both of the parties mutually add an intention against some essential blessing of marriage, and it can also mean that one party alone has an intention against an essential property of the marriage contract whereby he refuses, with an explicit act of his will, to become obliged to observed that essential property. In both cases the act of the will, when reduced to an agreement against some essential property of the marriage contract, invalidates the contract. Yet in another sense the expression "to reduce something to an agreement" becomes reflected even by the positive contrary act of the will.[104] Wherefore, Coronata says:

> Ad hoc ut habeatur vera et propria simulatio requiritur et sufficit ex expressa Codicis sanctione positivus voluntatis actus excludens aliquam, idest vel unam, ex proprietatibus essentialibus matrimonii, id est aliquod ex tribus matrimonii bonis, nempe vel bonum prolis vel bonum fidei vel bonum sacramenti. Non est vero necesse ut exclusio contractus aut proprietatis seu boni essentialis deducatur in pactum aut ut conditio apponatur.[105]

---

[103] Regarding the case of total simulation, whether it was done by one of the parties through malice or not, Gasparri noted: "... cum consensum excludat, matrimonium reddit prorsus nullum. At vero, huiusmodi fictio seu simulatio in foro externo non praesumitur, sed probanda est certis argumentis quia *'nemo existimandus est dixisse quod non mente agitaverit,'* (D. (33.10) (7.2)) et in dubio standum est pro valore matrimonii etiam in foro interno. Quod si simulatio revera adfuit, sed in foro externo non probatur, matrimonium erit reipsa nullum in foro interno, sed in foro externo habebitur validum."—*De Matrimonio,* II, n. 817, pp. 38-39.

[104] Cf. Coronata, *De Matrimonio,* n. 459, p. 617.

[105] *Loc. cit.*

It is true that the more ancient practice of the Rota had required that the intention against an essential property be made the matter of an agreement.[106] The more modern jurisprudence, however, admits also that a simple, positive contrary act of the will can invalidate consent and marriage. Thus, in a decision of the 10th of May, 1916, the Sacred Roman Rota declared: "...*fieri potest ut aliquis nupturiens ita contrahere sibi proponat, ut obligationes matrimonii essentiales, aut etiam unam ex illis expresse et positive reiiciat, quo in casu, etiam absque pacto, matrimonium nullum est.*"[107] This principle comes from the natural law; it is not required that an intention of excluding an essential property appear in the formula of the matrimonial contract or be added as a condition or be made the object of an express agreement to render the marriage contract null.[108]

The presumption of law contained in canon 1086, § 1, makes it necessary that if there was such an internal exclusion, it must be clearly proved, and this will be difficult to do unless the condition was expressed. Chelodi recognized that the earlier jurisprudence of the Rota seemed to require that the intention be *"deducta in pactum,"* but observed: *"serius admissum est hoc non esse necessarium,"*[109] citing Rotal decisions to support his view. But, as he concluded:

> . . . quod iudici inquirenti vix aut ne vix quidem constare
> potest intentionem contrahendi matrimonium solubile prae-

---

[106] Cf. S.C.S.Off., (Basniae), 2 dec. 1680—*Fontes*, n. 755; S.C.S.Off., (Mission. Capuccin.), 23 iul. 1698—*Fontes*, n. 761.

[107] S.R.Rota, Parisien., nullitatis matrimonii, coram R.P.D. Gulielmo Sebastianelli, die 10 maii 1916 — *Acta Apostolicae Sedis, Commentarium Officiale* (Romae, 1909—), IX (1917), 33 (hereafter cited *AAS*).

[108] "Quod principium, cum ex ipso naturali lege defluat, semper valet quando reapsa matrimonium initum est cum intentione excludendi proprietatem eius essentialem, quin necesse sit ut intentio appareat in formula nuptiali, aut tamquam conditio sit apposita, aut sit in pactum deducta. Unde declarationes quae in contrarium afferuntur, et quae videntur non admittere nullitatem nisi fuerit intentio in pactum deducta, intelligendae sunt de praesumptione iuris quae contra limitatum consensum militat, cum externe absolute contrahitur."—Chelodi, *De Matrimonio*, n. 116, p. 141.

[109] *Loc. cit.*

valuisse voluntati generali matrimonium ineundi, prout a Christo vel ab Auctore naturae institutum est . . . nisi probetur intentionem istam (contrahentem) in pactum deduxisse, seu consensum sub hac conditione, et non aliter, praestitisse.[110]

Thus it is seen that one who contracts with the intention of not being obligated under one of the essential notes of the contract has two acts of the will, both indeed positive, but reciprocally also contrary: he wills to contract marriage and at the same time wills not to by excluding or limiting the obligation and the right arising from that contract. This latter intention destroys the former, or, if one prefers, they cancel each other, so that there is no matrimonial consent.[111] In such a supposition, one sees present a true act of the will, and not simply an interpretative intention, or only a speculative error. The contracting party has an explicit and positive intention of not obligating himself or herself in any way; the person will not give or receive the right over the body, or that right in its relationship to the acts which serve the generation of offspring, or in a perpetual and exclusive manner, proposing internally, but in a positive fashion, to have the will to contract marriage but to exclude from it an essential property. In this case the contracting party on the one hand wills marriage and on the other hand excludes it. This restriction of consent excludes matrimonial consent.[112]

This positive intention is not a speculative error of the intellect. Here there is present a positive act of the will; in a simple error there is no act of the will, either internal or external.[113] The simple error will not invalidate the marriage contract because there is, on the part of the contracting party, a single, sufficient act of the will. When there is a positive intention not to oblige oneself to the matri-

---

[110] *Loc. cit.*

[111] Cf. Chelodi, *loc. cit.*

[112] Cf. Gasparri, *De Matrimonio*, II, n. 825, pp. 44-45; Sipos, *Enchiridion Iuris Canonici*, § 131, p. 500; Wernz-Vidal, *Ius Matrimoniale*, n. 461, p. 594; Vlaming, *Praelectiones Iuris Matrimonii*, Art. IV, p. 389.

[113] "Non sufficit e contra ad simulationem proprie dictam constituendam simplex error circa essentiales matrimonii, quia simpliciter errans nihil vult nec interne nec externe."—Coronata, *De Matrimonio*, n. 459, p. 618.

monial contract or its essential properties, there are two acts of the will, mutually destructive of one another.[114]

Necessarily, as has been previously stressed, if the speculative error of the intellect proceeds beyond the domain of a simple error and leads to an act of the will which expresses itself in a contrary intention, the marriage is invalid. Thus, for example, if one in error about the perpetual nature of marriage foresees that he cannot lead a peaceful life with his intended wife and therefore wills to be bound by the contract of marriage only for a time, this error antecedes the contract. Furthermore, there is added to this error an act of the will which positively excludes an essential property of marriage and, in consequence of this added act of the will, the marriage is null. Similarly, if one laboring under such an error, when interrogated about his opinion regarding the indissolubility of the marriage before he enters it, declares that he will seek a divorce if there are dissensions after the marriage, the contract is likewise invalid.[115]

Regardless of the particular blessing which might be the object of the simulation with the intention of not contracting at all, or of not obligating oneself to the contract, the contract will be invalid. In the case of the third kind of simulation, when one intends to contract and to be obliged to the resultant rights and duties from that contract, but intends not to fulfill those rights and duties, there does not result the same identity of invalidating effects with reference to the three blessings of marriage, offspring, fidelity and indissolubility. It is possible in such a case that one does not have the intention of fulfilling the contract. If this intention is directed against the blessing of offspring or of fidelity, the marriage is valid. The reason is that the blessings of offspring and fidelity are essential to the marriage contract as to their obligatory nature; they are not essential as to the execution thereof. However, as regards the blessing of indissolubility, this distinction does not obtain. Who-

---

[114] "Exinde facile intelligitur curnam simplex error contra substantiam non irritet, dum intentio sese non obligandi irritat; quia scilicet in casu simplicis erroris habetur unicus et sufficiens voluntatis actus; in casu autem intentionis sese non obligandi habentur duo actus voluntatis, se mutuo destruentes; unde illic adest consensus matrimonialis; hic non adest."—Gasparri, *De Matrimonio,* n. 825, p. 45.

[115] Cf. Coronata, *De Matrimonio,* n. 459, p. 618.

ever intends a dissoluble marriage, even as to execution, does not contract at all.[116]

One can, then, in regard to the *bonum prolis* and the *bonum fidei,* have the intention of entering the contract and obliging oneself thereto and, at the same time, have the intention of not fulfilling these obligations, v.g., by not rendering the conjugal debt when reasonably requested, or by committing adultery. Such a marriage will still be valid. The reason is that the intention of entering a contract and thereby becoming obliged to the performance of certain acts can coexist with the intention of violating the obligations assumed.[117] This same distinction cannot be held for the third blessing of marriage; a true marriage cannot be conceived as dissoluble. If one wills to marry he must will that this union be permanent, or he does not intend to enter a true marriage.[118]

The intention of not observing fidelity to one's marriage partner need not be an intention against indissolubility. Thus, one could intend to contract a true, perpetual contract of marriage and nevertheless intend to cast aside his wife under certain circumstances and

[116] "Solummodo quoad bonum sacramenti (quoad indissolubilitatem) non potest fieri distinctio inter matrimonialem obligationem at huius adimplementum. Qui positive intendit inire matrimonium solubile, nulliter contrahit."—Sipos, *Enchiridion Iuris Canonici,* § 131, p. 501.

"... qui matrimonium vult, debet velle perpetuum et qui solubile intendit non vult matrimonium."—Wernz-Vidal, *Ius Matrimoniale,* n. 462, p. 595.

[117] "Nam bona fidei et prolis non pertinent ad esse matrimonii, sed ad eius usum; at esse rei non pendet ab usu suo."—Chelodi, *De Matrimonio,* n. 117, p. 142.

"Si contrahens habet intentionem contrahendi et sese obligandi, sed non implendi seu iura matrimonialia servandi, intendens, e.g. abusum matrimonii, adulteria, procurationem abortus futurae prolis etc. ipse quidem graviter peccat, sed matrimonium valet. Nam intentio contrahendi et sese obligandi stare utique potest cum firmo proposito obligationem violandi; illa autem intentio constituit consensum et satis est pro validitate contractus." — Gasparri, *De Matrimonio,* n. 823, p. 46.

"Ad valorem enim consensus et matrimonii sufficit ut contrahentes mutuo sibi tradant et acceptent ius in corpus . . . usus vero iuris non est ad valorem consensus et matrimonio necessarius quamvis iam ante nuptias sit ab utroque aut ab alterutra parte exclusus."—Coronata, *De Matrimonio,* n. 463, p. 622; cf. also: *op. cit.,* n. 464, p. 625.

[118] Cf. *supra,* p. 52; also: Chelodi, *De Matrimonio,* n. 117, p. 152; Coronata, *De Matrimonio,* n. 465, p. 626.

accept another woman. In such a case one would certainly sin against the requisite fidelity to one's marriage obligations, but the contract could be valid. When, however, one intends to reserve to himself the power to reject his wife, so that he is free from the bond of marriage, he does not intend an indissoluble union and therefore does not contract a true marriage, since the will to contract a union is erased by the will to reject the essential element of perpetuity.[119]

The placing of such a contrary intention is not to be restricted only to those who labor under errors about the indissoluble nature of marriage. Also a Catholic party who would enter marriage within the Church and intend by a positive act of his will to obtain a divorce under certain circumstances and to enter a new marriage, even though a merely civil one, would reject the perpetual nature of the contract and thus vitiate his consent and nullify his marriage contract.[120]

Canon 1086 treats of a positive act of the will, whereby an essential note of the marriage contract is excluded. Without a positive act of the will there can be no true and proper consent.[121] The positive act of the will as it is referred to in the cited canon 1086 should not be confused with a condition added to the marriage contract. The latter is dealt with in canon 1092. The act of the will to which canon 1086 makes reference is an *absolute* will to enter a dissoluble union; it is not a conditional contract. It is true that the intention to exclude the essential object of the consent can be and frequently

---

[119] "... qui intendat sibi reservare potestatem in certis adiunctis mulierem abiciendi, ita ut maneat liber a vinculo ipsius, cum non intendat contrahere vinculum indissolubile, seu ius perpetuum et exclusivum tradere et acceptare, is invalide contrahit, cum voluntas contrahendi matrimonium elidatur per voluntatem ipsi contrarium circa idem objectum."—Wernz-Vidal, *Ius Matrimoniale,* n. 462, pp. 595-596. Cf. also De Smet, *De Matrimonio,* n. 533, p. 468.

[120] If, however, such a Catholic party intended only freedom under the civil law, knowing and intending that he will remain bound by the indissoluble bond before God and the Church, his intention does not vitiate his consent, since it does not exclude the perpetuity of the marriage contract. Cf. Coronata, *De Matrimonio,* n. 465, p. 627.

[121] "Importat actum positivum, sine quo verus et proprie dictus consensus ne concipi quidem potest."—Cappello, *Summa,* Vol. II, n. 377, p. 348.

is expressed by words which also designate a conditional consent, but a conditional consent does not depend on the words or formula used; it depends rather on the intention of the agent.[122]

Having considered these defects of the marital consent, on the part of the intellect or of the will, one can see that there is a certain discrepancy in the use of the expression "conditions against the substance of marriage." For, if a person intends a conditional consent to marriage, he wills marriage (true marriage as established by God), but intends that this contract of marriage produce its effect only on the verification of the condition attached to his consent. If, however, a person intends to exclude some essential property of marriage, there is no true, marital consent present, and because of this defective consent the marriage is invalid *ab initio,* not because some condition was not subsequently verified. Therefore, it is impossible to have a *condition,* properly so called, that is contrary to the substance of marriage added to a true will to marry.[123]

There is, nevertheless, justification for the common usage of this expression *"conditions against the substance"* in the writings of canonists, since the term is consecrated by such usage in the Decretals and in the Code of Canon Law, and especially because such intentions are commonly expressed grammatically in conditional words or phrases. Such a condition is not the equivalent of an intention *deducta in pactum,* in spite of the fact that they may be expressed in similar ways. The condition is a "circumstance elevated to effect a suspension of the act," whereas the intention *deducta in pactum* in a marriage consent "is a diseased consent of the will."[124]

---

[122] "Evidens quidem est quod ille qui vult matrimonium dissolubile, vult absolute matrimonium; sed quia vult absolute id quod reapse non datur, proprie nihil efficit. Nihilominus *absolute* vult tamen rem (quae non datur) et propter hoc non habetur matrimonium *sub conditione.* Errori autem ansa praebetur, quia voluntas excludens obiectum essentiale consensus matrimonialis exprimi potest et reapse non raro exprimitur aut mente concipitur verbis quae etiam designant conditionem . . . Utrum autem matrimonium sit absolute initum an sub conditione non dependet a verbis aut formula, sed a re et intentione quae verbis exprimitur."—Vlaming, *Pralectiones Iuris Matrimonii,* Art. III, *Corollarium,* p. 389.

[123] Cf. Timlin, *Conditional Matrimonial Consent,* Chap. XI, pp. 124-126.

[124] Timlin, *op. cit.,* p. 128.

With these preliminary notions clearly in mind, one may next proceed to the consideration of conditional consent, and specifically of the conditions which are contrary to the perpetual bond of marriage.

CHAPTER IV
CONDITIONAL CONSENT

ARTICLE I. NATURE OF CONDITIONS IN GENERAL

A condition, considered in the broad sense, is any circumstance from which the parties to a contract want the existence of their obligation in the contract to depend. In its strict sense, a condition is an uncertain future event from which, by the will of the parties to a contract, the validity of their consent to the contract depends.[1] In this study the question concerns the conditions in the broad sense. It is defined as *"circumstantia actui adiecta ex qua ipse actus pendet."* [2] A condition attached to a consent may be generally identified grammatically by means of such introductory words as if, until, while, as long as or unless. A condition is accordingly to be considered as any circumstance to which the consent in the marriage contract is attached in such a way that the validity of the marriage contract depends on the fulfillment or the non-fulfillment of that circumstance. This dependency may be reflected in two ways: the fulfillment of the condition may put an end to the contract, in which case it is called a *resolvent* or *voiding* condition, or the fulfillment of the condition may cause the contract, held in abeyance until then, to take effect, and in this case it is called a *suspensive* condition.[3]

For a true understanding of the meaning of condition, one must distinguish it from similar modifications of the consent, *mode, cause, demonstration* and *time clause.* These are qualifications of the consent, added by the parties, which do not essentially affect the content of the consent.[4] A *mode* (*"modus"*) is an obligation at-

---

[1] "Conditio lato sensu est circumstantia a qua partes exsistentiam ipsius obligationis contractus pendere volunt. Sensu stricto, est eventus non certo futurus a quo pendet, e voluntate contrahentis, vis ipsius consensus."—Vermeersch-Creusen, *Epitome Iuris Canonici* (3. ed., 3 vols., Mechliniae—Romae: H. Dessain, 1927-1928), Vol. II, n. 379, pp. 235-236.

[2] Payen, *De Matrimonio*, II, n. 1725, p. 125.

[3] Ayrinhac-Lydon, *Marriage Legislation in the New Code of Canon Law*, n. 223, p. 220.

[4] Timlin, *Conditional Matrimonial Consent*, p. 80.

79

tached to an already completed matrimonial contract and binding in justice on the other party to the contract.[5] A *cause* ("*causa*") is the expression of the motive because of which the party entered the contract.[6] A *demonstration* ("*demonstratio*") is a description of the person, or the indication of some quality which is either actually existing or at least is thought to exist in the other person.[7] A *time clause* ("*dies*") is the application of a *terminus a quo* or a *terminus ad quem* to the contract; it designates some event, not yet existing but certain to happen, upon which the obligation of the contract will begin or end.[8] The effect which these modifications may have on the validity of the matrimonial contract, if they affect the essential element of indissolubility, will be discussed in a further chapter. Suffice it to say here that the first three are added to a contract already essentially complete, and, as such, they differ specifically from conditions.

The authors from the time of the Glossators to the Decretals had distinguished various types of conditions.[9] The differences between the types of conditions can best be understood from a consideration of the names given them by the authors. For the sake of clarity, one may from the beginning sum up these types according to the following division:

I. Suspensive or resolvent

II. Reckoning with the past, with the present or with the future

III. Impossible or possible $\left\{\begin{array}{l}\text{necessary}\\\text{or}\\\text{contingent}\end{array}\right.$ $\left\{\begin{array}{l}\text{enterprising}\\\text{or}\\\text{causal}\\\text{or}\\\text{composite}\end{array}\right.$

[5] "Modus est onus adiectum contractui matrimoniali iam perfecto et ex iustitia ab altera parte ferendum."—Payen, *op. cit.*, II, n. 1725, p. 125.

[6] "Causa est expressio ipsius rationis ad nuptias ineundas moventis."—Payen, *loc. cit.*

[7] "Demonstratio est descriptio personae seu significatio alicuius qualitatis in comparte reapse existentis aut saltem pro existente habitae."—Payen, *loc. cit.*

[8] "Cum dies (terminus) adiicitur, designatur factum nondum existens, at certo futurum, a cuius existentia obligatio initium aut finem habebit."—Vermeersch-Creusen, *Epitome Iuris Canonici*, Vol. II, n. 379, p. 236.

[9] Cf. *supra*, pp. 21-23.

IV. Moral or immoral

V. Against or not against the substance of marriage

From the viewpoint of whether the circumstance to which the consent is attached is to give rise to the obligation or to connote an ending of that obligation, the condition is suspensive or resolvent. A suspensive condition is illustrated in the following clause: "I marry you *if my father consents"; a resolvent condition is evident in the following: "I propose to live in marriage with you *until I find someone wealthier."*

From the viewpoint of the time to which the conditional element is referred, a condition may look to the present, to the past or to the future. Thus, a condition reckons with the present in the formula: "I marry you *if you are a virgin";* with the past in the formula: "I marry you *if you have already begun instructions in the faith,"* and with the future in the formula: "I marry you *when you will begin taking instructions in the faith."*

From the viewpoint of the condition's eventual potentiality for fulfillment, a condition may be possible or impossible. An example of the former would be: "I marry you *if you will learn to dance,"* and an example of the latter would be: "I marry you *if you will touch the sky."* Conditions which are possible are either necessary or contingent, according as their fulfillment is sealed as something altogether inescapable or emerges as something completely optional. Thus the proposition, "I marry you *if the sun rises tomorrow,"* gives expression to a necessary condition, while the proposition, "I marry you *if my father consents"* reflects a dependence on the free will of a third person and is thus contingently possible.

A contingently possible condition is further distinguished from the viewpoint of whether the fulfillment of the condition depends on the free will of the parties themselves, or at least one of them, or whether its fulfillment depends on the free will of someone other than the parties, or on some contingent circumstance out of their control. Under this consideration, a condition may be characterized as enterprising (*potestativa*) if it depends for its fulfillment on one or both of the parties to the contract. It is causal if it depends on the will of someone else or on the occurrence of some contingent event over which the parties have no control. Finally, it is of a composite or mixed character if it depends for its fulfillment partly on the free will of the parties and partly on someone or something else. An enterprising condition is exemplified in the proposition: "I marry you *if you will take instructions in the faith;*" a causal condition in: "I marry you *if my father consents,*" and a condition of composite or mixed nature is: "I marry you *if you become a Catholic,*" which contingent fact depends not only on the will of the party to the contract, but also on the acceptance of that party's profession of faith by the representative of the Church.

From the viewpoint of the lawfulness of the attached condition, a condition may be moral (*honesta*) or immoral (*turpis*). Thus a condition is moral if it conforms to human and divine laws; it is immoral if it is opposed to these laws. A moral condition is stated in the following: "I marry you *if you will take instructions in the faith;*" an immoral condition in the following: "I marry you *if you will have an operation to preclude the bearing of children.*" A condition, whether in itself moral or immoral, can be against the substance of marriage or not against the substance of marriage (*repugnans vel non repugnans substantiae*). An example of an immoral condition which is not contrary to the substance of marriage would be: "I marry you *if you will murder your mother;*" a moral condition not against the substance of marriage would be: "I marry you *if you will take instructions.*"

A condition against the substance of marriage can militate against the marriage itself in its very essence, as in the formula: "I marry you *if I retain completely all rights over my body,*" or it can be placed against an essential property of marriage. Thus a condition could militate against the blessing of children (*bonum prolis*): "I marry you *with the proviso that you cannot claim the right to have marital relations in the normal manner;*" it could militate against the blessing of fidelity (*bonum fidei*): "I marry you *if I may keep another woman,*" and it could militate against the blessing of indissolubility (*bonum sacramenti*): "I marry you *if I can have a divorce when I want one.*"[10]

[10] Any of these conditions given previously may reckon with past, present or future realities or contingencies, with the exception of the conditions which militate against the substance of marriage, which must always look to the future and not to the past or present if they are to beget any effect on the contract. Thus

There are authors who mention other types of conditions, but these are not truly conditions in the sense explained. Thus some authors speak of a condition which is implicitly attached to the consent. However, there can be no such thing as an implicit condition, as Coronata observes:

> Conditio implicita haberi nequit, quia ipsa positivum actum voluntatis importat ideoque actum explicitum. Poterit utique haberi conditio posita per actum mere internum voluntatis, quae tamen in solo foro interno vim habere potest, nisi forte indirecte et ipsa ex casus adiunctis et circumstantiis probari possit.[11]

Similarly, some authors discuss tacit conditions or conditions *of law* (*conditiones iuris*), which are said to obtain when some condition is held to be present in a juridical contract by operation of the law itself, as illustrated in the following: "I marry you *if there is no diriment impediment to our marriage,*" or "I marry you *if you are not my sister.*" These are not true conditions, and correspondingly the contract is not a conditional one. These are intrinsic to the contract, whereas a condition in the true sense must be extrinsic.[12] Thus Timlin calls these, not conditions, but "terms for describing the requirements necessarily presupposed by the essential nature of a juristic act."[13]

Another type of condition mentioned by some authors is the *interpretative* condition, namely, if a person would not have entered the contract if he had known that the other party lacked such and such a quality. This is merely an antecedent error that indeed gives rise to the consent (*causam dans contractui*), but which does not enter into the act of the will, and therefore has no effect juridically on the consent.[14]

Schmalzgrueber stated: "Vel talis conditio repugnans substantiae vel bonis matrimonii apponitur de praesenti aut de praeterito vel de futuro. Si de praesenti aut de praeterito, matrimonium eius appositione non vitiatur; sed ea existente valet, illa non existente nullum est, quia tales non sunt conditiones quae tempus praeteritum vel praesens respiciunt."—*Ius Ecclesiasticum,* Lib. IV, tit. V, n. 115.

[11] *De Matrimonio,* Cap. V, n. 493, pp. 665-666.

[12] Cf. Coronata, *De Matrimonio,* Cap. V, n. 493, p. 670.

[13] *Conditional Matrimonial Consent,* p. 85.

[14] "...de facto non existat. Nec enim attenditur quid factum fuisset in determinata hypothesi, sed quid revera factum sit."—Coronata, *op. cit.,* n. 493, p. 670.

To complete the consideration of the nature of conditions in general, one should in addition note the following aspects. As may be seen from the consideration of the various types of conditions, only the contingent condition which reckons with a future eventuality is a condition in the strict sense: all other conditions are such only in the broad sense.[15] A condition which for its verification must look to the past or present, a condition which reckons with a future necessary event and also a condition impossible of achievement are called conditions only in a broad sense, since they are not such as to effect the suspending of the consent.[16]

That a consent be conditional it is not necessary that the condition be placed in connection with the actual exchange of consent in the juridical form of marriage. If a person has formed an actual intention to enter the matrimonial contract in a conditional manner, and this intention then virtually continued until the mutual exchange of consent, the consent itself must be regarded as conditional. The reason is that a condition, once placed, is presumed to remain in force until it is revoked.[17]

Both the intellect and the will operate in the conditional consent: the intellect considers the circumstances which are the object of the condition, and presents them to the will; the will gives consent to the contractual obligations only dependently, making the matrimonial consent depend on the fulfillment of the condition. This does not mean, however, that these are two distinct acts; it is one act, but an act which is not simple, but conditional.[18] If these two factors are present in the consent, it does not matter how the con-

---

[15] "...the condition properly so called is that whose happening is contingent in the future, for the nature of a true condition is to suspend the effect of the transaction and its resulting obligations and to make that act exist or not according to the existence or not of the condition in reality."—Timlin, *Conditional Matrimonial Consent*, p. 84.

[16] Cf. Coronata, *op. cit.*, n. 493. p. 670.

[17] Cf. Coronata, *op. cit.*, n. 493, p. 665.

[18] "Conditio duo importat: respectum intellectus ad circumstantiam illam quae est ipsum conditionis obiectum et actum voluntatis quo negotium iuridicum, matrimonium, dependenter ab illa circumstantia initur. Actus tamen voluntatis, ad negotium seu matrimonium necessarius et appositio conditionis, ut diximus, non sunt duo actus distincti, sed unicus actus non purus nec simplex, sed conditionatus."—Coronata, *loc. cit.*

sent was expressed, or whether the grammatical form of the expression was properly conditional. In each case the accompanying circumstances must be considered, since it is the will of the parties that makes the consent conditional or absolute.[19]

ARTICLE II. CONDITIONS NOT AGAINST THE SUBSTANCE OF MARRIAGE

Canon 1092 establishes the laws concerning the effect of conditions attached to a matrimonial consent:

Conditio semel apposita et non revocata:
1° Si sit de futuro necessaria vel impossibilis vel turpis, sed non contra matrimonii substantiam, pro non adiecta habeatur;
2° Si de futuro contra matrimonii substantiam, illud reddit invalidum;
3° Si de futuro licita, valorem matrimonii suspendit;
4° Si de praeterito vel de praesenti, matrimonium erit validum vel non, prout id quod conditioni subest, exsistit vel non.

Since the only pertinent section of this canon as applicable to the present study is number 2° which points to a condition that is contrary to the substance of marriage, there will be only a very brief consideration of the other conditions, those namely which are not against the substance.[20]

A. CONDITIONS RECKONING WITH THE FUTURE

1. NECESSARY, IMPOSSIBLE AND IMMORAL CONDITIONS

Conditio semel apposita et non revocata, si sit de futuro necessaria vel impossibilis vel turpis, pro non adiecta habeatur.

This first part of canon 1092, based on the teaching of Gregory

---

[19] "Verum ad iudicium ferendum de conditione matrimonio apposita non tantum ad expressiones a partibus adhibitis attendendum est, sed potius ad ipsam partis aut partium voluntatem quae ex omnibus casuum singulorum adiunctis colligi potest."—Coronata, *loc. cit.*

[20] A full study of all these conditions will be found in Father Timlin's treatise, *Conditional Matrimonial Consent,* already cited several times. In this brief survey of the conditions which do not militate against the substance of marriage, there is much reliance on this study.

IX in his Decretal *Si conditiones*,[21] states it as a presumption of law that any of these conditions attached to a contract, as long as they do not militate against the substance of marriage, are to be treated as if they had not been added to the contract at all. This is, of course, only a *praesumptio iuris,* established because of the favor in law which marriage enjoys, and, as such, it must always give way to proof of the contrary. Therefore, if the parties can adduce definite proof that they seriously intended their consent to depend on the fulfillment of such conditions, such conditions cannot be disregarded as not attached. On the contrary, the impossible condition thus added to the contract will make the consent inefficacious; the necessary condition will make the marriage valid only when the necessary event is verified; immoral conditions will have the same effect of suspending consent as do moral ones. The serious intent alleged in such conditions must, however, be proved in some external manner, or the presumption that they were not added at all will stand in the external forum of the Church.[22]

In canon 1092, 1° it is only the conditions that reckon with the future that are so to be considered as *"non adiectae";* conditions reckoning with the present or the past are considered in canon 1092, 4°, where it is declared that the validity of the marriage will depend on whether or not the condition is fulfilled.

If a condition which reckons with a necessary, future event is intrinsically necessary by the nature of the thing or by a disposition of the law, the marriage is valid at once. The same is true if the condition is one that is extrinsically necessary, such as the rising of the sun on the following day. This condition is already determined in its cause and is correspondingly considered as already existing. This is not so when the condition is seriously placed as a *conditio sine qua non;* in this case it suspends the marriage. A condition which so reckons with a future, necessary event is sometimes equivalent to the determination of a requisite point of time, as would obtain if one said: "I marry you *when* the sun rises." The marriage is then effected only when the sun rises. These possible variants of

---

[21] C. 7, X, *de conditionibus appositis in desponsatione vel in aliis contractibus,* IV, 5.

[22] Cf. Timlin, *op. cit.,* p. 137.

a necessary, future condition must always be determined from a consideration of the individual cases.[23]

In a similar fashion a condition which reckons with a future, impossible event is presumptively to be regarded as not really attached to the contractual consent. Depending on the object of the condition, such a condition may look to something that is impossible metaphysically, *ex natura rei,* as when nature itself invariably bars its very existence; to something which is impossible physically in as much as it is beyond the powers of any individual to achieve or to perform; to something that is impossible morally, in as much as it is beyond the powers of the specific individual who is involved, or to something which is legally impossible because the law prohibits its fulfillment. Such conditions dealing with future, impossible events are fundamentally (*per se*) to be treated as not seriously attached to the consent and the contract is thus equivalently an absolute contract.[24]

Immoral conditions, as long as they do not militate against the substance of marriage, are similarly considered in law as not attached to the consent. In a doubt about the intention of the one who invokes such a condition, the presumption of the law directs that the invoked condition is not to be regarded as a serious one. This is clear from the teaching of the Decretal *Si Conditiones* of Gregory IX and the wording of canon 1092. The basis for the presumptive non-admission of immoral conditions in the matrimonial contract is that the very invoking of them would incite a person to sin.[25]

2. Licit Conditions

Conditio semel apposita et non revocata, si sit de futuro licita, valorem matrimonii suspendit.

A true and licit condition has the effect of suspending the validity of marriage so that no bond of marriage is created until that licit condition has been fulfilled. Marriage is thus not made by the veri-

---

[23] Cf. Timlin, *op. cit.,* p. 144.

[24] All this is applicable in the external forum only; the decision as to the validity in the internal forum depends in full reality on the will of the one who attached the condition to his consent. Cf. Timlin, *op. cit.,* pp. 151-152.

[25] Cf. Timlin, *op. cit.,* p. 158.

fication of the condition alone, but by the consent given conditionally, upon the verification of that condition. No renewal of consent is necessary for the validity of the marriage, for the original consent continues. This is certainly so in a conditional contract, since it is true even in a marriage contracted invalidly because of an impediment.[26]

An honorable and licit condition which looks to the future suspends the formation of the marriage in both the internal and external forum. It must be understood, however, that, though the parties to the contract assume the obligation to fulfill their contract once the condition is verified, they have no such obligation to verify that condition when that condition is enterprising, that is when it is dependent on the will of the parties for its fulfillment or verification.[27]

B. Conditions Reckoning with the Past or the Present

Conditio semel apposita et non revocata: si de praeterito vel de praesenti, matrimonium erit validum vel non, prout id quod conditioni subest, exsistit vel non.

All conditions which look to the past or to the present, of whatever type, are regulated by the rule stated in this section four of canon 1092. Impossible conditions which look to the past or to the present, therefore, are not ruled out as are the impossible conditions that reckon with the future, but they are judged according to section four, and a marriage thus contracted is valid or invalid depending on whether the condition is or is not verified.[28]

Immoral conditions that look to the past or to the present are not considered as not attached to the consent, but the marriage is valid if the condition is or was verified; it is invalid if the condition

---

[26] "Etsi matrimonium invalide ratione impedimenti initum fuerit, consensus praestitus praesumitur perseverare, donec de eius revocatione constiterit."—Canon 1093. Cf. also Timlin, *op. cit.*, pp. 98-102.

[27] Cf. Timlin, *op. cit.*, p. 176.

[28] "The marriage is valid if the condition [that looks to the past] is verified, otherwise it is null, since the consent is attached to the fulfillment of the condition." . . "The marriage is valid at once if the condition [that looks to the future] is verified, otherwise it is null from the start."—Ayrinhac-Lydon, *Marriage Legislation in the New Code of Canon Law*, pp. 224-225.

is not or was not verified.[29] The principal reason for the Church's legal presumption in immoral conditions looking to the future is that they incite to sin. Immoral conditions which refer to the present or the past, however, do not incite to sin, but simply suppose a sinful fact. Thus the condition: "I marry you if you are a thief," although immoral, supposes the fact of sin already committed, and the condition: "I marry you if you have killed your father," immoral as it is, likewise supposes a sin which has been committed. Neither of these incite to later sin, as does an immoral condition that looks to the future. Therefore, such conditions fall under the provision of canon 1092, 4°.[30]

With this brief appraisal of the various types of conditions which are not against the substance of marriage, one can pass on to a study of those conditions which look to the future and are, at the same time, contrary to the substance of marriage.

ARTICLE III. CONDITIONS AGAINST THE SUBSTANCE OF MARRIAGE

A. CONDITIONS RECKONING WITH THE FUTURE

Conditio semel apposita et non revocata: si [sit] de futuro contra matrimonii substantiam, illud reddit invalidum.

In section two of canon 1092, there is mention of that element in the marriage consent which is the specifically proper topic of this study. One must recall here what has been explained previously, namely that the term *condition*, if it seeks to denote a circumstance attached to the consent contrary to the substance of marriage, is essentially a misnomer, since a consent thus conditioned is an essentially defective marital consent, for marriage cannot exist without its substance. For this reason it is really not a consent to marriage at all.

One must recall further that this study deals, not with intentions contrary to the marriage, but with the intention under the formality of a condition contrary to the substance of marriage. A contrary intention is much wider in extent than a condition, for a positive intention may be defined as a resolute act of the will whereby a person

---

[29] Cf. Timlin, *op. cit.*, p. 154.
[30] Cf. Timlin, *op. cit.*, p. 158.

takes a definite stand regarding the object in question.[31] This intention of the will may be expressed in other ways, namely by a positive contrary act of the will (canon 1086, § 2), or by a total or a partial simulation.

There is, indeed, a distinction between a positive contrary act of the will as considered in canon 1086 and a condition attached against the substance of marriage as discussed in canon 1092.[32] Total simulation likewise differs from a conditional consent, since total simulation is no consent at all but an apparent consent only. In simulation there is an act of the will which is psychologically complete, but which does not effect a true marriage for the reason that it is not a true consent, and *"matrimonium facit partium consensus"* as canon 1081 defines. Conditional consent, on the other hand, is a true consent, but, because the effecting of marriage is made dependent on the fulfillment of a condition, it is not a pure and simple consent.[33] It is therefore evident that the exclusion of one of the essential obligations of marriage need not be in the form of a condition to invalidate the contract. It is sufficient for this that there be an explicit contrary act of the will.

As a matter of fact, it will be much easier to prove the existence of a contrary condition than that of a positive, contrary intention. A person who makes his consent depend on a condition which is against the substance of marriage may be unaware of the nullity of that marriage, whereas, "one cannot conceive of a case of total simulation in which the simulator did not have the intention of simulating."[34] Under this aspect, a conditional consent, though unlike total simulation, is like partial simulation, which exists when the person's marital consent is directed towards something which does not possess at the same time both the essence and the essential qualities of marriage.[35]

In treating of a conditional consent which is contrary to the sub-

---

[31] Griese, *The Marriage Contract and the Procreation of Offspring*, p. 55.

[32] Cf. Vlaming, *Praelectiones Iuris Matrimonii*, Art. III, *Corollarium*, p. 389.

[33] Courtemanche, *The Total Simulation of Matrimonial Consent*, The Catholic University of America Canon Law Studies, n. 270 (Washington, D.C.: The Catholic University of America Press, 1948), p. 31.

[34] Courtemanche, *op. cit.*, p. 18.

[35] Courtemanche, *op. cit.*, pp. 24 and 32.

stance of marriage, the writer includes the essence of marriage and its essential qualities of unity and indissolubility. The reason for this is evident from canon 1081, § 2: *"Consensus matrimonialis est actus voluntatis quo utraque pars tradit et acceptat ius in corpus, perpetum et exclusivum, in ordine ad actus per se aptos ad prolis generationem."* These three essential elements of the marriage contract are, as has been said, summed up in the three essential blessings of marriage: the *bonum prolis,* the *bonum fidei* and the *bonum sacramenti.* Accordingly consideration will be given here to the conditions contrary to the *bonum prolis* and to the *bonum fidei.*

1. CONDITIONS CONTRARY TO THE PRIMARY END OF MARRIAGE

Matrimonii finis primarius est procreatio atque educatio prolis.

This declaration of canon 1013, § 1, identifies the *bonum prolis;* any condition which is placed against the procreation of children or against the raising of the children born to the marriage, in the sense which will be explained, will invalidate that marriage. The procreation of children involves the giving and accepting of the marital right to those acts which of their nature are fitted as a means for the procreation of children. The education of the children thus born, in so far as it is an essential obligation which the marital consent cannot positively exclude, includes the physical and moral raising of the children . . . sustenance, protection, support and, at least, a minimum of training in morality.[36]

The obligation which, with reference to the primary end of marriage, arises from the marital consent will therefore comprehend the rendering of the sexual act, once it has been requested, in a proper manner according to its nature as intended by the Creator. It likewise precludes any and all right to do anything illicit to impede the generation and raising of children. It does not necessarily preclude the *fact* of so acting.[37]

There is indicated here a strong distinction between the condition against the *bonum prolis* and an intention which runs counter

---

[36] Cf. Timlin, *Conditional Matrimonial Consent,* p. 293.

[37] Cf. Timlin, *op. cit.,* p. 294.

to that *bonum*. It is evident that if a party to the contract excludes marriage itself, or the full right to the acts proper thereto, or the unity or indissolubility of that contract by a positive act of his will, the marriage is null. It can be deduced from this that one who places a condition contrary to the blessing of offspring, and thus precludes this blessing or makes it impossible of fulfillment, provided that this is a real condition attached to the consent, invalidates his consent so that there is no marriage. This is so if the party adds this condition in such a way that, unless the stipulated preclusion is fulfilled, he withholds his consent to the marriage. This will not always be so in regard to an *intention* contrary to the *bonum prolis*.

A valid matrimonial consent is entirely compatible with the non-fulfillment of its obligation in regard to the blessings of offspring and fidelity, according to the dictum of St. Thomas: *"Bona fidei et prolis non pertinent ad esse matrimonii, sed ad eius usum; at esse rei non pendet ab usu suo."* [38] Thus, a man may positively intend to marry and, at the same time, have the positive intention of practicing onanism or of procuring abortions should the onanism fail in its desired effect, thereby violating the obligations he is now assuming in this contract of marriage. Accordingly, a couple could intend not to have children and so state their intention before the marriage, but still intend to marry in the true sense by giving and accepting full, conjugal rights and obligations, the while they intend not to fulfill these obligations. This is concisely expressed by Ayrinhac-Lydon:

> To contract marriage on condition that there will be no children or a limited number, if it means that the spouses do not give to each other the right to the acts apt for the generation of children, or that these rights are transferred only for a limited time, is to place a condition contrary to the essential object of the marriage contract and annuls it. If the condition meant that the rights are transferred but that they will not be used, we would be in presence of a lawful condition and hence one not contrary to the essence of marriage. Marriage contracted under

---

[38] *Summa Theologica,* Pars III, q. 49, art. 3.

condition of practicing onanism will be null and void according as the condition implies the refusal of marital rights or is only a sinful condition, e.g., provided I can abuse marriage.[39]

In this matter, therefore, one must always ask whether the contrary intention in the will of the parties is to be reduced to a condition *sine qua non,* or is it a contrary intention directed against the fulfillment of obligations truly assumed in the matrimonial consent. The marriage contract is thus invalid if the parties reserve the *right* to practice onanism or to procure abortion, should a child be conceived, or to kill born or unborn children in any way. The acceptance of these obligations, however, along with the intention to abuse the rights of marriage does not invalidate the consent.

It is similarly not of the essence of the marriage contract that the begetting of offspring or the exercise of the act of intercourse be expressly willed or intended. Indeed, the positive intention of the contracting parties may be not to consummate the marriage; such was the marriage of St. Joseph and the Blessed Mother. In every marriage, nevertheless, there must be the giving and the accepting of the right (*tradere-acceptare ius*), so that each has the dominion over the body of the other for those acts suited for procreation. If this right is not given and accepted, there is no true marriage contract.[40]

Canon 1081 refers to this marriage right as a *ius perpetuum,* and therefore it is not postulated that the *ius* be excluded completely. If the *right* to the proper use of the marriage act is excluded for any time, as, for example, "until we are better established in life" or "after we have had one or two children", the marriage is invalid from the beginning. (Again the *right* must be excluded, not just the *fulfillment* of the right.) The right, as a *ius perpetuum,* cannot be excluded for a day or for an hour, since such a right cannot be given partially.[41]

In this matter especially there is the common admonition of the

---

[39] *Marriage Legislation in the New Code of Canon Law,* pp. 226-227.
[40] Cf. Timlin, *loc. cit.*
[41] Cf. Timlin, *op. cit.,* p. 300.

authors, as well as the warning from the Sacred Roman Rota,[42] not to be hasty in judging a marriage invalid because of a condition contrary to the *bonum prolis,* for the judgement must be based on the expressions used by the parties in their designation of the condition. If they simply wish to refuse to fulfill the obligations which they actually assumed and intended to be binding, their marriage is valid. Both parties consider themselves truly married and bound by the laws of marriage regarding their conjugal obligations.

The obligations which the parents of children assume radically in the marriage contract are summed up in the words of canon 1113: *"Parentes gravissima obligatione tenentur prolis educationem tum religiosam et moralem, tum physicam et civilem pro viribus curandi, et etiam temporali eorum bono providendi."* If the intention of refusing to assume any of these obligations is added as a modification of the consent by means of a mode, cause or demonstration, or if the parties intend indeed to assume these obligations, but intend also not to fulfill them, the marriage is valid. If these obligations are excluded in consequence of a true condition, the marriage is invalid because of a condition contrary to the substance of marriage in the exclusion of the *"educatio prolis"*, as it is demanded in canon 1013, § 1. There are authors who hold that the modifications added to the contract, such as the agreement to raise the children in heresy or without baptism, do not inherently (*per se*) invalidate the contract, even if they were placed as conditions to the consent, but are to be ruled out as immoral conditions. As Timlin points out, however, *"educare"* in the sense of canon 1013, § 1, is an essential of the marital consent.[43]

The writer feels that notice must be taken that this is so only in

---

[42] "At caute distinguendum est inter ipsam matrimonialem obligationem et huius adimplementum. Hoc enim potest contingere, ut contrahens ita sit animo comparatus, ut vere et serio velit contrahere et se obligare, et tamen praevidens matrimonii abusum, v.g. onanismum, pravam habeat voluntatem hoc delictum permittendi, aut etiam committendi, et ita suas obligationes violandi."—S.R.Rota, *Parisien.,* Nullitatis matrimonii, coram R.P.D. Gulielmo Sebastianelli, die 10 maii, 1916—*AAS,* IX (1917), 33.

[43] *Op. cit.,* p. 311. To pursue this question, which lies beyond the scope of this treatise, one may consult the references to be found in Timlin, pp. 310-311.

the sense that the parties to the marriage may not, by a positive intention, *exclude the obligation* of raising their children. It is not true in the sense that the parties must positively intend the *"educatio prolis"* as a component part of their marital consent. While it is true that the education of the children is part of the primary end of marriage, as canon 1013, § 2 clearly states, it is not equally included in the extension of the matrimonial consent as defined by canon 1081, § 2. One may distinguish between the *bonum prolis* in the strict sense, i.e. *"ius in corpus, perpetuum et exclusivum, in ordine ad actus per se aptos ad prolis generationem,"* and the *bonum prolis* in the broad sense, i.e. *"procreatio et educatio prolis."* The former must be intended as an integral part of the matrimonial consent; unless the consent extends to this, there is no marriage. Although the latter may not be excluded by a positive, contrary intention or condition which refuses to be bound by the *obligation* of the *bonum prolis* in the broad sense, this is not necessarily *included* as an integral part of the marriage contractual consent, as defined by canon 1081, § 2. The parties need only intend positively to give and to accept the mutual right to each other's body for those acts which are, by nature, suited for the procreation of children, a mutual right which is perpetual and exclusive. Nothing more is required for a valid consent.

As to the possibility of honorable conditions against the substance of marriage in as much as they preclude the exercise of the rights of marriage, authors dispute whether such conditions do or do not invalidate marriage. The condition commonly discussed is that of a vow of perpetual chastity, or an agreement to live in a state of perpetual chastity. Their opinions depend on whether or not they accept a distinction between the *right* to marital relations and the *use* of that right. The better opinion is that the moral character of the condition is irrelevant as regards the substance of marriage; if in any given instance the radical dominion over the body is excluded, the marriage contract is null. Renunciation of the actual use and exercise of this radical dominion will not destroy that contract. One can receive a right to the use of something and yet not exercise that right, without losing it. The marriage is valid if only the exercise of the right is excluded and the right itself is given and accepted.[44] Thus, as Timlin, concluded rightly, "the pact obliging one or both *not to give* the *debitum* invalidates if the parties excluded or did not receive the *radical* right to *demand,* otherwise the pact is not against the substance." [45] In view of this, if one were to extract a promise or vow in the form of a condition, e.g. "I marry you, provided that you promise (or vow) not to ask for your conjugal rights (i.e. which you possess) during the Lenten season," the right is given without limitation and a promise or vow is exacted that one will not use the right thus possessed. Such a condition is not against the substance of marriage, since the essentials of the *bonum prolis are safeguarded.*[46]

2. Conditions Contrary to the Unity of Marriage

Essentiales matrimonii proprietates sunt unitas et indissolubilitas, quae in matrimonio christiano peculiarem obtinent firmitatem ratione sacramenti.

From this disposition of canon 1013, § 2, one derives the canonical law on the essential nature of the unity of the matrimonial contract, by which is meant the fidelity which each party to a marriage contract is obliged to render to the other. Contrary to the exclusiveness of the marriage bond are polyandry, polygyny, whether these be simultaneous or successive, as well as the right to have intercourse with someone other than the partner. The unity of marriage means, therefore, the marriage of one man with one woman, and the *bonum fidei,* which is the result of this exclusive nature, connotes the right and the obligation of fidelity imposed on each party to the contract. Theologians commonly teach that polyandry (union of one woman with several men) is contrary to the primary precepts of the natural law, and that polygyny (union of one man with several women) is in opposition to the secondary precepts of the natural law.[47]

The *bonum fidei* means not only that the couple have the obligation of rendering the marriage debt to each other, but also that

[44] Timlin, *op. cit.,* pp. 319-320.
[45] *Ibid.,* p. 326.
[46] *Ibid.,* p. 328.
[47] Cf. Ayrinhac-Lyon, *Marriage Legislation in the New Code of Canon Law,* p. 5.

they have no right to intercourse with another party. Any condition which excludes this obligation is contrary to the substance of marriage in its essential quality. There results from this blessing a mutual obligation: to render the debt, to live together in love, to forego any marriage with another while both live, and to refrain from any act of illegitimate affection for another while the marriage lasts.[48] Therefore, a condition of polygyny, polyandry or adultery, when reserved as a right proves contrary to the essence of marriage; the actual commission of adultery subsequently does not in and of itself run counter to the essence of marriage, but rather militates against its integrity. The same distinction that exists in the matter of the *bonum prolis* between the obligation assumed in the contract and the fulfilling or non-fulfilling of that obligation also stands in the matter of the *bonum fidei*. In fact, all the principles and their applications that were noted in regard to the *bonum prolis* apply equally to this blessing of fidelity.[49]

B. Conditions Reckoning with the Past or the Present

To complete the consideration of the conditions which militate against the substance of marriage, one may restate the legislation on such conditions when they look to the past or to the present. Canon 1092, 4° relates to all such conditions, whether they are contrary to the substance of marriage or not. Every condition referring to the past or the present will be determined by whether the condition is fulfilled or not, unless it can be reduced to a condition which substantially affects the marriage in the future. An example of such a past condition which substantially affects the contract in the future is: "I marry you, if you *have procured* condoms to use *in the future* as a *right* in our marital relations." In a case such as this, the defect of the consent comes, not from the fulfillment of the past event, but from the positive act of the will, here and now, which excludes an essential element of the marriage.[50]

---

[48] Cf. Timlin, *op. cit.*, p. 331.

[49] Cf. Timlin, *op. cit.*, p 333. For examples of such conditions against the *bonum fidei* which would invalidate the contract of marriage, cf. Timlin, *op. cit.*, p. 332.

[50] Cf. Timlin, *op. cit.*, p. 337 and p. 340.

It remains now to consider the condition contrary to the indissolubility of marriage, the *bonum sacramenti,* and the effect that such an intention will exercise on the validity of the marriage thus conditionally contracted.

CHAPTER V
THE INVALIDATING CONDITION AGAINST INDISSOLUBILITY

Article I. The Importance of the Question

In the present day the matter of conditions attached to the marriage contract, in line with which that contract is to be dissolved by the civil authority, upon the will of the parties, should subsequent events prove the marriage burdensome, can be of the utmost importance. It is true that the condition of dissolving the marriage is not of frequent occurrence when both parties are Catholic, but it may appear at times in mixed marriages, and it is not uncommon in marriages between non-Catholics. The reason derives from the spreading error that the marriage contract is a civil contract only, a social contract, which can be ended whenever the parties so desire.

To emphasize the serious import of the question, it is only necessary to quote the words of Pope Pius XI in the Encyclical Letter on Christian Marriage:

> . . . let it be repeated as an unchanged and inviolable fundamental doctrine that matrimony was not instituted or restored by man but by God; not by man were the laws made to strengthen and confirm and elevate it but by God, the Author of Nature, and by Christ our Lord by whom nature was redeemed, and hence these laws cannot be subject to any human decrees or to any contrary pact even of the spouses themselves. This is the doctrine of Holy Scripture, this is the constant tradition of the universal Church, this is the solemn definition of the sacred Council of Trent, which declares and establishes from the words of Holy Writ itself that God is the Author of the perpetual stability of the marriage bond, its unity and its firmness.[1]

Notwithstanding this fact, the Holy Father further stated:

> And now considering that the third blessing, which is that

---

[1] Pius XI, litt. encycl., *Casti connubii*, 31 dec. 1930—*AAS XXII* (1930), 541. The translation of this encyclical is taken from the *completely revised* translation based on the translation sent out by the N. C. W. C. News Service and published as *Christian Marriage, Encyclical Letter (Casti Connubii) of Pope Pius XI* (New York: The America Press, 1942), p. 2 (hereafter cited as *Christian Marriage*).

of the "Sacrament", far surpasses the other two, we should not be surprised to find that this, because of its outstanding excellence, is much more sharply attacked by the same people. They put forward in the first place that matrimony belongs entirely to the profane and purely civil sphere, that it is not to be committed to the religious society, the Church of Christ, but to civil society alone. They then add that the marriage contract is to be freed from any indissoluble bond, and that separation and divorce are not only to be tolerated but sanctioned by the law; from which it follows finally that, robbed of all its holiness, matrimony should be enumerated amongst the secular and civil institutions.[2]

The daily increasing facility of divorce has led to widespread social evils which are a matter of grave concern to men of conscience. Still, as the Holy Father pointed out:

The advocates of the Neo-Paganism of today have learned nothing from the sad state of affairs, but instead, day by day, more and more vehemently, they continue by legislation to attack the indissolubility of the marriage bond, proclaiming that the lawfulness of divorce must be recognized, and that the antiquated laws should give place to a new and more humane legislation.[3]

Some would go even further, as the Pontiff declared:

Other, taking a step further, simply state that marriage, being a private contract, is, like other private contracts, to be left to the consent and good pleasure of both parties, and so can be dissolved for any reason whatsoever.[4]

In the United States, the permissibility and frequency of divorce are well known. The Constitution of the United States left complete authority over marriage and divorce legislation to the several states.[5] Thus the Domestic Relations Law, section 10, of New York, defines marriage as "...a civil contract, to which the consent of

---

[2] *Christian Marriage*, p. 24; cf. *Casti connubii—AAS XXII* (1930), 569.

[3] *Ibid.*, pp. 26-27; cf. *Casti connubii—AAS*, XXII (1930), 572.

[4] *Ibid.*, p. 27; cf. *Casti connubii—AAS*, XXII (1930), 573.

[5] Richard V. Mackay, *Laws of Marriage and Divorce Simplified*, 2. ed. by Irving Mandell, Legal Almanac Series (New York: Oceana Publications, 1954), p. 7.

the parties . . . is essential." To the concept that marriage is a civil contract, the courts have added that marriage is also a "status" to which the state is a third party.[6] Because of the acceptance of marriage as a civil contract alone, all the States of the United States have adopted divorce statutes in their statute law. As grounds for divorce, the States accept causes of action ranging from the sole cause of adultery in New York State to as many as twenty grounds in the State of Kentucky.[7] Although the courts still insist that a divorce suit must represent a contest, a large percentage of divorces are amicable and simply reflect some arrangement between the parties. In the eyes of the law, the court must be satisfied that there has been a genuinely contested divorce action, before any decree may be entered. Referring to this, Mackay admits: "In view of present day procedure, this attitude seems absurd and hypocritical."[8]

Going far beyond this doctrine of the state that the marriages of its citizens are of social significance, the belief is becoming more and more widespread that marriage is a private contract, which should be left to the determination of the parties for its dissolution. Favoring this is the "Omnibus Provision" of many statute codes, which allow courts of equity great leeway in accepting reasons for the dissolution of the bond, giving relief for many causes not listed in the statutes.[9]

Commenting on this extension of the viewpoint of statute law, an eminent sociologist says:

Although civil legislation varies from state to state, the right to dissolve valid marriages is maintained by all states. Unless a marriage is contested, and only a small percentage are, the legal grounds on the basis of which the decree is granted are not significant, since it is an open secret that the great majority of such suits involve collusion. This distressing situation has arisen because of the disparity between accepted behavioural patterns and established legal norms. Divorce legislation is

---

[6] Mackay, *loc. cit.*

[7] Cf. Mackay, *op. cit.*, pp. 61-68, for a listing of the grounds for divorce in the various states.

[8] Mackay, *op. cit.*, p. 60.

[9] Mackay, *op. cit.*, p. 39.

based on the assumption that marriage is a socially significant institution and that the public interest requires some control over its formation and dissolution. Divorce is granted only to the "innocent" partner on proof that the "guilty" spouse has committed one of the offenses (legal grounds) specified by the law. Public opinion, on the other hand, tends to regard marriage as a private affair. Common law marriages are still recognized by a number of states. Few regulations governing the entrance into marriage are tolerated, and the courts have been forced to acquiesce in the popular demand for the equivalent of divorce by mutual consent.[10]

With the prevalence of this lax opinion, it is not surprising that divorce statistics have shown a steady rise in the United States and throughout the world.[11] Since this is so, it is evident that a great proportion of our people today look upon marriage as a dissoluble, temporary contract. With most this is a speculative error, an *error iuris,* and probably in the great majority of cases it remains speculative, so that they do not make it part of their contractual consent. In many other cases, however, this speculative error about indissolubility may lead to the expressed intention of not contracting in any but a dissoluble fashion, or to the addition of a condition to the contract that the marriage will be terminated should it subsequently prove onerous to either or both of the parties.

It is of great importance, therefore, that one establish clearly the factors of such conditions against the *bonum sacramenti,* the blessing of indissolubility, which attaches to marriage. In the following articles we shall try to show what is required in a conditional consent regarding the perpetual bond to invalidate that consent.

Article II. The Nature of Indissolubility

The indissolubility of marriage is indicated in various ways in the Code of Canon Law. The Code delineates the essential properties of marriage:

[10] John L. Thomas, *The American Catholic Family* (Englewood Cliffs, N. J. Prentice-Hall, Inc., 1956), Chap. XI, pp. 321-322.

[11] In 1959, in the United States alone, 395,000 divorces were granted, according to the latest available statistics of the Public Health Service of the Department of Health, Education and Welfare of the United States Government.—*The World Almanac and Book of Facts* (New York World-Telegram, 1962 ed.), p. 309.

Essentiales matrimonii proprietates sunt unitas et indissolubilitas, quae in matrimonio christiano obtinent firmitatem ratione sacramenti.[12]

The Code indicates, as well, that the matrimonial consent must
include the element of permanence:

Consensus matrimonialis est actus voluntatis quo utraque
pars tradit et acceptat ius in corpus, perpetuum et exclusivum,
in ordine ad actus per se aptos ad prolis generationem.[13]

Furthermore, the Code also requires that the note of permanence
must at least be known by the contracting parties for a valid consent:

Ut matrimonialis consensus haberi possit, necesse est ut contrahentes saltem non ignorent matrimonium esse societatem
permanentem inter virum et mulierem ad filios procreandos.[14]

Although simple error regarding the note of indissolubility will
not vitiate the marriage consent,[15] it is the law of the Code that a
positive act of the will excluding indissolubility,[16] or also a conditional, prospective consent which precludes indissolubility will nullify that consent.[17] Among the effects of a valid marriage is that of
an indissoluble bond:

Ex valido matrimonio enascitur inter coniuges vinculum natura sua perpetuum et exclusivum.[18]

This bond, in a ratified and consummated marriage, is so firm that

. . . nulla humana potestate nullaque causa, praeterquam morte,
dissolvi potest.[19]

Accepting, then, the existence and importance of the element of
indissolubility in marriage, one may rightfully inquire what is the
specific nature of indissolubility before one discusses the conditions
that militate against it.

---

[12] Canon 1013, § 2.
[13] Canon 1081, § 2.
[14] Canon 1082, § 1.
[15] Canon 1084.
[16] Canon 1086, § 2.
[17] Canon 1092, 2°.
[18] Canon 1110.
[19] Canon 1118.

The basis for the indissolubility of the marriage bond is the natural law. The contrary proposition, namely: *"Iure naturae matrimonii vinculum non est indissolubile, et in variis casibus divortium proprie dictum auctoritate civili sanciri potest,"* was condemned by Pope Pius IX.[20] From this it follows that the opposite is true; civil authority can never grant a true divorce from the bond of marriage even for its unbelieving subjects.[21] The precepts of the natural law, however, are of two kinds, according to the measure of the efficacy of these precepts, *primary* and *secondary*. The primary precepts are the ones: *"quae natura absolute exigit, quia sine illis ordo moralis redditur impossibilis,"* and the secondary are the ones: *"in quae natura valde quidem inclinat, quia sine illis ordo moralis est minus perfectus, quae tamen hypothetice exigit."* [22]

It is evident that the moral order is not rendered impossible by a dissoluble union (e.g. in a childless marriage or when the children have already been raised). A temporary marriage does not necessarily thwart the primary end of marriage. Therefore, indissolubility is not required as a *primary* precept of the natural law.[23] The dissolving of the marriage bond at the will of the parties themselves, however, is against the primary precepts of the natural law. A free union of the parties, by which each or both could dissolve the bond at will, is evidently against the principal end of marriage, which re-

---

[20] Cf. *Syllabus, seu Collectio Errorum Modernorum*, n. 67—Denzinger, *Enchiridion Symbolorum Definitionum et Declarationum de Rebus Fidei et Morum* (ed. 28., Friburgi Brisgoviae: Herder, 1952), n. 1767.

[21] "Unde sequitur matrimonii vinculum ipso naturali iure esse aliquo modo indissolubile, et auctoritatem civilem nunquam divortium proprie dictum sancire posse, ne pro subditis quidem infidelibus."—Gasparri, *De Matrimonio*, II, n. 1123, p. 200.

[22] Noldin-Schmitt, *Summa Theologiae Moralis*, Vol. I, n. 113, p. 122.

[23] "... omnimoda indissolubilitas vinculi non est ex praeceptis primariis legis naturae, tum quia dari potest casus quo ea minime excludat finem principalem matrimonii, procreationem nempe et educationem prolis, e.g. si matrimonium est sterile aut filii educationem iam receperint; tum quia obstat in V.T. libellus repudii permissus hebraeis, in N.T. privilegum fidei, et in genere potestas Romani Pontificis dispensandi in matrimoniali vinculo."—Gasparri, *De Matrimonio*, II, n. 1124, p. 200.

quires permanence in parental life.[24] The *complete* indissolubility of the matrimonial bond derives then from the secondary precepts of the natural law. This is so because the fulfillment of the primary end of the contract and the fuller and easier implementation of the secondary end of mutual help require an indissoluble bond in marriage. Indissolubility is therefore necessary for the perfection of the moral order of marriage.[25]

To understand what are the effects of this bond one has but to consider the benefits which flow from indissolubility. In the words of Pope Pius XI:

Indeed, how many and how important are the benefits which flow from the indissolubility of matrimony cannot escape anyone who gives even a brief consideration either to the good of the spouses and the offspring or to the welfare of human society. First of all, the spouses possess a positive guarantee of the enduringness of this stability which that generous yielding of their persons and the intimate fellowship of their hearts by their nature strongly require, since true love knows no end. Besides a strong bulwark is set up in defense of a loyal chastity against incitements to infidelity, should any be encountered from within or from without; any anxious fear lest in adversity or old age the other spouse would prove unfaithful is precluded and in its place there reigns a calm sense of security.

Moreover, the dignity of both man and wife is maintained and the mutual aid is most satisfactorily assured, while through the indissoluble bond, always enduring, the spouses are warned continuously that not for the sake of perishable things nor that

[24] "... solubilitas vinculi ex mera voluntate unius, aut etiam utriusque coniugis est contra praecepta primaria legis naturae. Aliis verbis, unio libera, ut aiunt, qua coniuges possunt se separare et ad alia vota transire, quandocumque alteruter voluerit, aut etiam uterque consenserit, est contra praecepta primaria legis naturae; nam manifeste contraria est fini principali matrimonii seu educationi prolis, quae requirit diuturnum parentum convictum."—Gasparri, *ibid.*, n. 1125, p. 200.

[25] "Praeterea omnimoda indissolubilitas vinculi in genere est ex praeceptis secundariis legis naturae, cum per eamdem melius consulatur bono prolis, et plenius ac facilius obtineatur finis secundarius matrimonii, mutuum scilicet adiutorium, etsi in nonnullis casibus particularibus hoc perpetuum iugum durum videri possit." — Gasparri, *op. cit.*, II, n. 1126, p. 201.

they might serve their passions, but that they might procure one for the other high and lasting good have they entered into the nuptial partnership, to be dissolved only by death. For the training and education of children, which must extend over a period of many years, it is splendidly adapted, since the grave and long enduring burdens of this office are best borne by the united efforts of the parents. Nor do lesser benefits accrue to human society as a whole, for experience has taught that unassailable stability in matrimony is a fruitful source of virtuous life and of habits of integrity. Where this order of things obtains, the happiness and well-being of the nation are safeguarded. As the families and individuals are, so also is the State, for it is made up of them even as a body is of its members. Hence those who vigorously uphold the inviolable stability of matrimony make a real contribution both to the individual welfare of huband, wife and offspring, as well as to the general welfare of mankind.[26]

The opposite of indissolubility is divorce, which is defined as a: *"solutio matrimonii sive quoad vinculum, sive manente vinculo saltem quoad torum vel cohabitationem, sive per declarationem nullitatis."* [27] Divorce is of two categories. In a complete divorce the objectively extant bond of marriage becomes truly dissolved, but in an incomplete divorce, the bond of marriage itself remains firm and intact, though there is a separation "from bed and board". A complete or true divorce, then, reflects the dissolution of a previously existing and valid bond of marriage. An official declaration of the non-existence of any previous, valid bond of marriage is not properly a divorce. Such a declaration simply reflects continuous nullity from the very start of the supposed marital contract. But the incomplete divorce points either to a perpetual or to a temporary separation, dependently on whether the cause for the separation is permanent or transitory. A temporary separation in turn is partial, if it refers only to a separation from the common bed, or total, if it

---

[26] *Christian Marriage*, p. 12; cf. *Casti connubii—AAS*, XXII (1930), 553-554
[27] Wernz-Vidal, *Ius Matrimoniale*, n. 620, pp. 782-783.

refers to a separation from a common cohabitation as well, that is from bed and board alike.[28]

Indissolubility can be characterized as *intrinsic* (internal) or as *extrinsic* (external). Intrinsic indissolubility consists in this that the marriage cannot be dissolved for any internal cause, or through the mutual consent of the contracting parties; extrinsic indissolubility means that the marriage cannot be dissolved by way of any external intervention, either divine or ecclesiastical.[29] This is explained in another way by Vlamnig:

> Auctores non raro distinguunt indissolubilitatem intrinsecam et extrinsecam, prout incapacitas solvendi respicit coniuges aut alios, scilicet viros auctoritate praeditos.[30]

Applying these definitions, one must claim for the marriage bond an *intrinsic* indissolubility by which it cannot be dissolved through the mutual consent of the parties, in consequence of the primary precepts of the natural law. The marriage bond is, furthermore, *extrinsically* indissoluble on the basis of the natural law in that it cannot be dissolved by any human authority. This extrinsic indissolubility is not absolute, since it does not oppose the primary precepts of the natural law.[31]

This can be seen clearly from the history of the doctrine. In the beginning of man, the primitive institution of marriage included the note of indissolubility, as is clearly evident from the words of *Genesis*: "Adhaerebit uxori suae et erunt duo in carne una." [32] Later it was made permissible for the Hebrews to use the bill of divorce, because of their hardness of heart. Then Christ revoked this per-

---

[28] Cf. Wernz-Vidal, *op. cit.*, n. 621, pp. 783-784.

[29] Noldin-Schmitt, *Summa Theologiae Moralis*, Vol. III, n. 518, p. 525.

[30] Vlaming, *Praelectiones Iuris Matrimonii*, p. 16, *nota*.

[31] "Matrimonium esse omnino indissolubile, dissolubilitate intrinseca, qua scilicet illud solvere nequeant communi consensu contrahentes, idque ex primariis iuris naturalis principiis."

"Matrimonium ex iure naturali etiam extrinseca indissolubilitate gaudere, quia generatim nulla humana auctoritate solvi potest. Haec tamen indissolubilitas extrinseca non est absoluta, quia non repugnat primariis iuris naturalis principiis solutionem matrimonii in certis et determinatis casibus permitti vel positiva concessione a Deo facta vel ipso iure naturali, praecisione facta a lege positiva divina aliud determinante."—Coronata, *De Matrimonio*, n. 611, p. 855.

[32] *Genesis*, II: 24.

mission to use the bill of divorce when He restored marriage to its primal firmness.[33] He further willed to add a special firmness to the marriage of the faithful by reason of its sacramental character, inasmuch as their marriage was to be a likeness of the union of Himself and His Church.[34] Because of this special firmness, a valid marriage of two baptized persons, once that marriage has been consummated by marital intercourse, is entirely indissoluble until death severs that bond.[35]

Thus, intrinsic indissolubility belonged to marriage from the beginning, although by God's permission the marriages among the Hebrews were dissoluble for certain causes. The marriage bond among Christians in the New Dispensation also may be extrinsically dissoluble, in the sense that God may dispense from the bond through His human representative on earth in certain cases. In the sense of the Church's teaching marriage is indissoluble, as a natural or as a sacramental contract, so that divorce is not just illicit but impossible. No man can dissolve that bond: the parties cannot do so, even by mutual consent; the state cannot, although it possess the authority of a perfect society. God, that Author of nature, who instituted that contract of marriage, can dissolve the bond of marriage, and He can, if He so chooses, share His power to dissolve with men.[36]

---

[33] Cf. Matthew, V: 31-32; Mark, X:11; Luke, XVI:18.

[34] Cf. Ephesians, V: 32.

[35] Cf. Gasparri, *De Matrimonio*, II, n. 1126, p. 201; Wernz-Vidal, *Ius Matrimoniale*, n. 622, pp. 784-792; De Becker, *De Sponsalibus et Matrimonio*, Sec. X, pp. 226-227; Coronata, *De Matrimonio*, n. 611, p. 855.

[36] "Matrimonium esse indissolubile docet Ecclesia Catholica, intelligens hac doctrina docere vinculi matrimonialis sive naturalis sive sacramentalis dissolutionem (seu divortium) non tantum esse illicitum sed etiam impossibilem. Inter homines nemo, neque alteruter coniux neque ambae partes consentientes et conspirantes, neque viri summa regiminis potestate in societate perfecta pollentes, est capax solvendi vinculum illud, de quo Christus solemniter locutus est: *'Ideo quod Deus coniunxit, homo non separet.'* Dico: *inter homines*. Matrimonium dicitur indissolubile sicut aegritudines quaedam dicuntur insanabiles. Sicut hoc ultimum non excludit Dei potestatem eas sanandi sua virtute divina, sic thesis nostra non excludit Deum, suo positivo interventu, posse aliquod matrimonium dissolvere." —Vlaming, *Praelectiones Iuris Matrimonii*, Art. II, p. 16.

Some of the cases in which God has determined to share His power of dissolving the marriage bond are: the non-consummated marriage of two baptized persons, or of one baptized and one not, when one of them makes solemn religious profession, or when, for a just cause, the Holy See has granted a dispensation from the bond (canon 1119); the legitimate marriage of non-baptized persons, even though consummated, which can be dissolved in favor of the faith, through the Pauline Privilege (canon 1120, § 1), and in general the marriage in which one of the parties is unbaptized, which likewise can be dissolved in favor of the faith, through a dispensation from the Supreme Pontiff.[37]

Since the indissolubility which is under consideration here applies to the marriages of the unbaptized as well as to those of the baptized, one cannot identify the *"sacramentum"* with the notion of sacramentality. In the marriage of infidels also there is a true *bonum sacramenti,* since, as Pope Pius XI stated quite clearly:

> This inviolable stability, although not in the same, perfect measure in every case, belongs to every true marriage, for the word of the Lord: *"What God has joined together let no man put asunder,"* since it was spoken of the marriage of our first parents, the prototype of every future marriage, must of necessity include all true marriages without exception.[38]

The perfection of this firmness comes through the sacramentality for Christians, a special firmness added to the *bonum sacramenti,* since, as canon 1013, § 2 states: *"in matrimonio christiano peculiarem obtinent firmitatem ratione sacramenti* [unitas et indissolubilitas]." Because of this special firmness a sacramental marriage, once it has been consummated by carnal intercourse, is so completely indissoluble that it cannot be dissolved even by divine power given to men, and much less can it ever be dissolved by any human author-

---

[37] "At simul Christus Dominus Ecclesiae suae concessit potestatem dissolvendi matrimonium non consummatum inter baptizatos, licet sacramenti dignitate praeditum; item matrimonium non consummatum inter partem baptizatam et partem non baptizatam, matrimonium etiam consummatum inter infideles in casu Apostoli et in genere matrimonium inter fideles in favorem fidei."—Gasparri, *De Matrimonio,* II, n. 1126, p. 202.

[38] *Christian Marriage,* p. 10; cf. *Casti connubii—AAS,* XXII (1930), 551.

ity. Before such a sacramental marriage has been consummated by intercourse it could be dissolved by divine power exercised through the instrumentality of the Roman Pontiff.[39]

The result of this is that the Roman Pontiff may declare a consummated marriage of baptized persons invalid because of some cause of nullity which was truly present, but if the union was valid to begin with, he cannot dissolve it for any reason.[40] Although the general principle remains true that marriage is always indissoluble intrinsically by reason of the primary precepts of the natural law, and it is equally indissoluble extrinsically in consequence of the secondary precepts of the natural law or of the positive divine law, there are certain determined exceptions to this extrinsic indissolubility. In view of these specific exceptions, the second part of this general principle in its strict interpretation is verified only in a *matrimonium ratum et consummatum*. Therefore, absolute indissolubility, both intrinsic and extrinsic, properly and exclusively belongs to a marriage which is ratified and consummated.[41]

The Schismatic Greeks and the Calvinists, as indeed most of the Protestant sects, reject this property of indissolubility. They base their reasoning on the words of Christ in Matthew, V: 32, and XIX: 9 . . . *"save on account of immorality"* and *"except for immorality."* Against this assertion it suffices to say that the Catholic tradition has always interpreted this text in the sense that adultery is a cause to put away one's wife by way of an incomplete divorce, namely by way of a separation, with the bond of marriage remaining firm and indissoluble. Therefore, any subsequent marriage un-

---

[39] "Codex matrimonio christiano specialem firmitatem seu indissolubilitatem tribuit ratione sacramenti. Per hoc indicatur sacramentalitatem matrimonii specialem firmitatem matrimonio tribuere, ita ut si matrimonium sacramentum consummatum sit non solum nulla humana auctoritate solvi possit, sed nec potestate divina hominibus concessa. Ad hoc autem ut haec specialis firmitas locum habeat requiritur ut haec duo elementa, nempe sacramentalitas et consummatio simul occurrant, alioquin matrimonium solvi poterit potestate divina Romano Pontifici concessa." — Coronata, *De Matrimonio*, n. 19, pp. 23-24.

[40] Cf. Gasparri, *De Matrimonio*, II, n. 1126, p. 201.

[41] Cf. Coronata, *De Matrimonio*, n. 611, pp. 855-856.

dertaken during the lifetime of the guilty spouse is not a valid union, but simply an adulterous one.[42]

Since the divine power to dispense from the indissoluble bond in *any* marriage, even in these few specific cases, has been given only to the Roman Pontiff, it follows that the civil power cannot grant a true divorce in the proper sense even for its unbaptized subjects.[43]

From this consideration of the nature and the effects of indissolubility, one will note that in the present study the matter of concern is the intrinsic indissolubility of the marriage bond. That bond can never be broken by the will of one or both of the parties to the contract, nor by the civil authority upon the parties' request. A positive act of the will which runs counter to this indissolubility will invalidate the contract, as will a condition which, when looking to the future, is placed against the *bonum sacramenti,* so that such a conditioned consent is no consent at all, and the substance of marriage is eradicated from the contract.

Article III. The Simple Intention Against Indissolubility

The Code declares clearly that any condition contrary to the attribute of indissolubility, which is essential to the substance of marriage, will invalidate that marriage when the set condition reckons with the future. Likewise a distinction must be made in general between an *intention* contrary to the substance and a *condition* which gives expression to that intention. The question that calls for consideration here, however, is whether there can be a true difference between the intention and the condition against indissolubility, or whether the simple intention contrary to indissolubility is equivalent to a condition.

The reason for this question is that almost all authors follow

[42] "Traditio catholica textum Matthaei semper interpretata est sensu quo ob fornicationem seu adulterium liceret quidem parti innocenti dimittere partem adulteram atque ab ea separationem petere a toro et cohabitatione, firmo manente vinculo coniugali ita ut matrimonium ab alterutro contractum habendum sit ut verum adulterium."—Coronata, *De Matrimonio,* n. 612, p. 857.

[43] "Exinde sequitur principem civilem etiam in casibus in quibus divortium proprie dictum non esset contra naturae legem, non posse illud sancire nec pro subditis infidelibus, cum nusquam legatur ipsi concessa potestas dispensandi a iure matrimoniali divino positivo."—Gasparri, *De Matrimonio,* II, n. 1126, p. 202.

Sanchez' opinion that one who contracts marriage must always intend the *bonum sacramenti,* at least implicity. This is not true of the other blessings of marriage in the same way as it is of the blessing of indissolubility. One can intend to contract marriage and to assume the obligations which flow therefrom, but at the same time one can intend not to fulfill these obligations as regards the *bonum prolis* and the *bonum fidei.* They cannot, however, contract a union while they propose not to observe it as indissoluble.[44]

One may be said to have the implicit intention to enter an indissoluble marriage whenever one has no contrary intention. It follows, therefore, that if one of the contracting parties has the intention to exclude indissolubility from the marriage, the marriage is null, even thought this intention is not externally manifested or expressed but only retained in the mind. Indissolubility is of the essence of marriage, as is evident from its definition; one who intends to enter a temporary marriage does not truly intend marriage at all.[45]

If one compares a condition with an intention, which is a positive act of the will, then, in regard to intentions and conditions which are against one of the blessings of marriage, one finds that the difference consists in this that the positive act of the will is a simple act which excludes one of the blessings of marriage absolutely, and therefore excludes marriage itself. In this case there is no marital consent at all, because such a positive act of the will is an actual or virtual intention contrary to the substance of marriage, whether this

---

[44] Cf. Coronata, *De Matrimonio,* n. 465, p. 626; Gasparri, *De Matrimonio,* II, n. 823, p. 46; Chelodi, *De Matrimonio,* n. 117, p. 142; Wernz-Vidal, *Ius Matrimoniale,* n. 462, pp. 595-596.

[45] "Sententia cui adhaereo docet contrahentem matrimonium debere saltem implicite intendere bonum sacramenti, quod evenit, quando non habet intentionem contrariam; non tamen esse opus, ut implicite intendat alia duo matrimonii bona; quare si haberet animum etiam corde retentum, adversum bono sacramenti, quia scilicet intenderet non contrahere matrimonium nisi ad tempus, non esset verum matrimonium. Si tamen haberet intentionem adversam aliis duobus matrimonii bonis, corde solo retentam, nec in pactum deductam, valeret utique. Probatur prior pars quia de ratione matrimonii est, vinculum esse perpetuum, et constat ex eius definitione tradita . . . Ergo, qui intendit matrimonium inire dissolubile et ad tempus, vere non intendit matrimonium, cum intentio adversetur essentiae."—Sanchez, *De Matrimonii Sacramento,* Lib. II, Disp. XXIX, n. 11, p. 116.

intention is externally manifested or is secretely retained in the mind. In either case it cannot coexist with a true matrimonial consent. A condition, on the other hand, presupposes the giving of consent by the contracting party, which consent, to become effective, looks to the fulfillment of a proviso in the future. When a condition is placed which is contrary to the substance of marriage, this consent is inefficacious because the consent cannot coexist with the incompatible contrary condition.[46]

It is thus evident that both in the intention contrary to the substance and in the condition contrary to the substance the same object is excluded, namely one of the essentials of the marriage substance. Some authors speak of two acts of the will in simulation, one willing marriage and the other willing not to marry;[47] others find this division superfluous. They see in every simulation a single act which excludes the contract of marriage, since the contracting party, when he intends to exclude from the contract any essential property of marriage, by that very fact intends to preclude marriage itself.[48]

In defending a twofold nature in a conditional consent, Coronata indicates that the contrary positive act of the will and the contrary condition do not differ in reality but rather in the manner in which they are expressed.[49] The same author admits that it is often difficult to discern whether the question at hand is one of a positive act of the will contrary to a substantial element of marriage or a condition against that substantial element. This he finds of small import, since he says that the solutions to questions of simulation

---

[46] Cf. Coronata, *De Matrimonio*, n. 511, pp. 696-697.

[47] Cf. Chelodi, *op. cit.*, n. 116, p. 140; Gasparri, *op. cit.*, II, n. 825, p. 48.

[48] "Nobis videtur in simulatione haberi unicus voluntatis actus, excludens matrimonium. Etiam quando pars intendit exclusionem alicuius proprietatis essentialis, eo ipso intendit excludere totum matrimonium, quia non vult contrahere illum contractum, qui est perpetuus et unus. Unde non possumus fingere contrahentem qui vult et simul non vult . . . in simulatione habetur unicus actus qui excludit matrimonium ipsum."—Fraghi, *De Conditionibus Matrimonio Appositis* (Romae: Officium Libri Catholici, 1941), p. 73.

[49] "Uterque actus, potius quam re, solo modo, differt, cum in actu positivo habeatur actus simplex, in conditione apposita actus habeatur veluti duplex cuius pars altera conditionem continens priorem partem quae actum positivum consensus matrimonialis contineret, destruit."—*De Matrimonio*, n. 511, p. 697.

and conditional consent are governed generally by the same principles.[50]

It is not necessary to suppose such a twofold consent; the opinion defended by Fraghi seems well founded. In the case of a positive act of the will which is contrary to the substance of marriage or one of its essential properties and in the case of a condition similarly opposed to the substance there are not two mutually destructive acts of the will. Rather, in either case there is one act of the will: in the positive contrary act of the will, some essential element of marriage is excluded by the will-act; in the case of a condition contrary to the substance of marriage, the consent is made to depend on the fulfillment of a juridical impossibility. In neither case is there a true marital consent. What one consents to in both these acts is not marriage, since, if indissolubility is excluded from the contract, marriage is excluded.

The essential difference between the intention and the condition is rather to be found in the manner in which they are treated in the external forum. The principal point of difference lies in the manner in which the opposition of each to the essential elements of marriage is manifested in the external forum.[51] It is less difficult to prove in the external forum that one or both of the contracting parties intended to exclude an essential obligation of marriage if the intention had been expressed as a condition to the contract, but this difference, as is evident, is incidental. For this reason whatever is said in regard to intentions which are contrary to indissolubility may generally be applied as well to conditions contrary to that essential element of marriage.[52] Since every condition must of necessity include an intention, it is of little importance to the validity of the marriage whether this intention was expressed absolutely by a positive act of the will or conditionally as a condition contrary to the substance of marriage.

One must keep in mind that only *positive* intentions can have any effect on the validity or invalidity of a marriage contract,

---

[50] "Solutiones autem quaestionum de simulatione ob actum positivum voluntatis contra aliquam proprietatem matrimonii et de conditione apposita contra matrimonii substantiam iisdem plerumque principiis reguntur."—*Ibid.*, p. 698.

[51] Griese, *The Marriage Contract and the Procreation of Offspring*, pp. 40-41.

[52] Griese, *loc. cit.*

whether in regard to the blessing of indissolubility or to either of the other two blessings of marriage.[53] In regard to the *bonum sacramenti* this positive intention, though only a virtual one, can still invalidate the marriage contract. If one or both of the parties intend, even with a virtual intention, to contract only a dissoluble and temporary marriage, this fact will suffice to invalidate that marriage, since no distinction can be made between the acknowledgment and the fulfillment of the obligation inherent in the perpetuity of the marriage bond. Inasmuch as marriage is indissoluble by its nature from the moment of mutual consent, any intention not to fulfill the obligation of perpetuity flowing from that consent is the same as an intention to exclude such an obligation.[54]

Neither the intention nor the condition contrary to indissolubility can affect the validity of the marriage unless they affect the contract in one of its essential elements. The intention to exclude indissolubility can affect the contract essentially from the mere fact that such an intention proceeds from a positive act of the will. This is evident from the above; there can be no distinction between the acceptance and the fulfillment of the obligation inherent in the perpetuity of the contract, since the fulfillment of this obligation belongs essentially to the marriage contract itself.

There are two specific canons in the Code of Canon Law which refer to positive acts of the will and to conditions which are contrary to the substance of marriage. Canon 1086, § 2, refers to internal consent, as is evident from § 1, of the same canon, and treats of positive acts of the will:

> § 1. Internus animi consensus semper praesumitur conformis verbis vel signis in celebrando matrimonio adhibitis.

> § 2. At si alterutra vel utraque pars positivo voluntatis actu excludat matrimonium ipsum, aut omne ius ad coniugalem actum, vel essentialem aliquam matrimonii proprietatem, invalide contrahit.

---

[53] Cf. Griese, *op. cit.*, p. 55.
[54] Cf. Griese, *ibid.*, p. 68

Canon 1092, 2°, when treating of conditional consent, declares that if a condition is added and not revoked, then

> 2° Si de futuro contra matrimonii substantiam [sit], illud reddit invalidum.

The relationship between an internal intention contrary to indissolubility and a condition contrary to indissolubility may be made clearer by means of a comparison between these two canons. There can be a matrimonial consent which is not conditional in form but which can certainly be reduced to the same thing in reality. The difference will, in such a case, be found in the fact that the validity of that marriage will be attacked in the external forum under the aspect of one canon rather than the other.

An example of such a consent would be: "I marry you, with the proviso that we retain the right to contract another marriage later if we so choose." This is certainly not a conditional consent with a condition that looks to the future, since the contracting parties do not make the existence of the present bond dependent on the fulfillment of a future event. Therefore, such a contract would not come under the terms of canon 1092, 2°. It is evident, nevertheless, that the intention expressed by such a consent is certainly the same as that envisaged by the codifiers of Canon Law in what they called a *"conditio de futuro contra substantiam matrimonii"* in canon 1092. The specific form of the intention expressed is covered by the terms of canon 1086, § 2, so that in this at least the two canons coincide.

The primary difference, then, will lie with this: in attacking the validity of a marriage entered into with such a state of mind on the part of the contracting parties, which canon will be applied? This will be determined by the form or the words used rather than by the reality expressed by such words. If the parties had contracted marriage with a positive act of the will that they would contract marriage only for the duration of a year or other specified time, the marriage is invalid by reason of canon 1086, § 2, and this canon refers to the case both *in fact and in form*. On the other hand, if the parties had contracted marriage with the condition added: "I marry you, with the proviso that we retain the right to contract another marriage after one year," *actually* they are doing the same thing, but the *form of expression* they used brings this case under the terms of canon 1092, 2°, and the invalidity of this marriage will be attacked under the terms of canon 1092.[55]

It is not to be thought that, these canons are not only much like each other but even are the same and do not differ at all. There is a great distinction, since canon 1086 deals with a simulation which is a completely different notion than that of a condition, which is the subject of canon 1092. In a case of simulation there is no will to contract marriage at all; while external expression is given of the intention to marry, internally something entirely contrary is intended. In a case of conditional consent, on the other hand, there is a will truly to marry, but this will is affixed to some circumstance which destroys the marriage contract.[56]

The effect of both simulation and conditional consent is the same in such an opposition to the indissolubility of the contract, namely the effect of nullity of the contract of marriage. The cause of this nullity, however, is different in each case. In simulation the will is not to marry or not to contract an indissoluble marriage; the will is *"antimatrimonialis"*, as it is called. In a case of a condition there is a will to marry, but this will to marry is affixed to some circumstance which, since it is contrary to the essential character of marriage, destroys the contract of marriage.[57]

Fraghi comes to the conclusion that canons 1086 and 1092 refer to two different questions, canon 1086 to that of simulation with a positive act of the will and canon 1092 to a question of a condition contrary to the substance of matrimony. He admits, as do most authors, that many questions arising from these two canons will often be similar, and that it will frequently be difficult to distin-

---

[55] Cf. Vlaming, *Praelectiones Iuris Matrimonii, Corollarium*, p. 396.

[56] "In simulatione nulla habetur voluntas contrahendi, quia dum externe aliquid affirmatur, interne omnino contrarium intenditur; in conditione vero voluntas adest, quae tamen alligata est alicui circumstantiae, quae hoc in casu, destruit contractum matrimonialem." — Fraghi, *De Conditionibus Matrimonio Appositis*, p. 71.

[57] "... in simulatione habetur voluntas negativa, voluntas scilicet quae interne non vult matrimonium, vel unam ex proprietatibus essentialibus; est voluntas antimatrimonialis, quam vocant; in conditione vero habetur voluntas, conditionalis quidem, sed semper voluntas, quae alligatur alicui circumstantiae, quae cum opponatur obiecto essentiali, destruit ipsum contractum matrimonialem."—Fraghi, *op. cit.*, p. 72.

guish when the question is one of simulation and when it is one of conditional consent. He does not admit that it is therefore licit to assume that canon 1086 can refer to a condition contrary to the substance, and that one can accordingly invoke it in settling a question of a conditional matrimonial consent.[58]

If one is, however, to make any distinction between an intention contrary to the *bonum sacramenti* and a condition contrary to the same blessing, then it seems to be a logical distinction and not a real one, in the light not only of the great weight of authority in favor of this opinion, but also of the evidence deriving from an intrinsic evaluation of the condition and the intention. Since every contrary condition is based on a contrary intention of the will, it seems that, in practice, they can be substantially identified as two aspects of the same thing. It is true, as Fraghi says, that the two canons involve two different aspects in that the cause for impugning the validity of the marriage is different in a case of simulation and in a case of conditional consent. This does seem, nevertheless, to be no more than a matter of the external forum, a *modus procedendi* in proving the invalidity, not an intrinsic difference in the will of the contracting parties in the two cases. In the case of a marriage alleged to be invalid because of a positive act of the will, the basis of proof will be found in canon 1086, § 2; in the case of a marriage alleged to be invalid because of an attached condition against the substance of marriage, the basis of proof will be in canon 1092, 2°.[59]

In the discussion that follows there will be treated the conditions contrary to the substance of marriage and, specifically, that condition contrary to the indissolubility of marriage, the *bonum sacramenti*. It is to be remembered that much of what will be said ap-

[58] Cf. Fraghi, *op. cit.*, pp. 73-74.

[59] This seems to be the finding of Dinus Staffa when he says: "Actus ergo positivus a conditione quoad substantiam non differt; in utroque casu habetur exclusio vel limitatio iuris; in utroque exclusio vel limitatio consensus; in utroque exclusio vel limitatio iuris procedit ab exclusione vel limitatione consensus tamquam immediatus et necessarius effectus. Cum enim ius e consensu oriatur, eatenus ius limitatur quatenus limitatur consensus, at consensus limitatio idem est ac conditio, ergo limitatio iuris idem est ac conditio."—*De Conditione contra Matrimonii Substantiam* (Romae: Apud Custodiam Librariam Pont. Instituti Utriusque Iuris, 1952), pp. 24-25.

plies to intentions as well insofar as the validity of marriage is concerned.

ARTICLE IV. THE INTERNAL CONDITION AGAINST INDISSOLUBILITY

It has been said again and again that a condition or an intention which is against the essential property of indissolubility in the marriage contract, if seriously intended in the giving of consent, invalidates the contract. The reason for this is that any such intention or condition indicates a positive act of the will which excludes some essential element of the marriage contract. When such an essential element is excluded by a positive act of the will, there is a true defect of matrimonial consent. *"Matrimonium facit partium consensus,"* as canon 1081, § 1, declares. When such an essential of the contract is excluded, therefore, there can be no marriage.

Although this is understood, if there is need of proof that such a positive act of the will was made, must such an act be expressed by the parties or party; must it be made the matter of an explicit stipulation attached to the contract, or will it suffice, if proof be available, that such an intention or condition was present in the will of one party? This question involves two factors: the favor that marriage enjoys in law, and the meaning and application of the *"deductio in pactum."*

Canon 1014 establishes the presumption in favor of the validity of marriage:

> Matrimonium gaudet favore iuris; quare in dubio standum est pro valore matrimonii, donec contrarium probetur, salvo praescripto canonis 1127.

This presumption intends to provide a particular protection, as it were, for marriage, because of the dignity of this sacramental contract and the stability required for it. The meaning of this *favor iuris* is this: once a marriage has been celebrated, the law of the Church holds that the marriage is a valid one, unless and until its invalidity has been proved, and it matters not whether the doubt that has arisen about its validity is one of law or one of fact.[60]

---

[60]"Semel celebratum matrimonium habendum est ut validum, donec contrarium probetur, sive dubium sit iuris sive facti."—Wernz-Vidal, *Ius Matrimoniale*, n. 44, p. 59.

The reasons in jurisprudence which justify this presumption are derived from the legal axiom: *"melior est conditio possidentis,"* since the marriage, once celebrated, is in possession, and from the importance to the *bonum prolis* and to the public good. It is most important for these last two that a marriage should not be broken up. This presumption of law holds for all marriages, for the baptized and for the unbaptized, for the internal as well as for the external forum.[61]

This favor of law guarantees that the Church's law will protect every apparent marriage against any attack on its juridical existence or on its validity, until it has been proved beyond doubt that it *is* invalid.[62]

It is not required that one have direct knowledge of the actual celebration of that marriage, for this favor of law will also extend to the state in which a man and a woman have lived for a long time, so that they and the community within which they live consider it a true marriage, even though they themselves and others cannot prove definitely that they once fulfilled all the requirements for a valid marriage.[63]

This favor of law is only a presumption, but it imposes a strong obligation on the parties to any marriage, even an invalid one that has been knowingly and maliciously entered into, not to attempt to contract another marriage until it has been definitely proved by certain arguments that the first marriage, now in possession until it is dislodged, was invalid.[64]

The only exception to this general principle of law that one must

[61] "Cuius iuridica ratio est quod matrimonium, certo celebratum, est in possessione et maxime interest boni prolis ac praesertim publici boni honestatis morum, ne matrimonia solvantur, quamdiu certo modo de eorum nullitate non constat. Quae ratio valet pro quolibet matrimonio etiam infidelium, et pro foro tam externo quam interno."—Wernz-Vidal, *loc. cit.*

[62] Cf. Vlaming, *Praelectiones Iuris Matrimonii*, Chap. IX, p. 47.

[63] Cf. Vlaming, *loc. cit.*

[64] "   ideoque, quantumvis ipsis partibus constet de eius nullitate, imo quantavis mala (etiam utriusque) fide nulliter initum, seu attentatum, ut tamen practice pro invalido haberi possit, nullitatis probatione in foro publico Ecclesiae indiget; adeo ut neutri parti ad novas liceat nuptias convolare, nisi sententia nullitatis prioris matrimonii a iudice ecclesiastico obtenta."—Vlaming, *op. cit.*, p. 48.

insist on the validity of the marriage in possession, when doubt arises, is made in favor of the faith for a case of the Pauline Privilege or the Privilege of the Faith. In these cases, because of the pre-eminence of the Faith, in a doubt of law or of fact the favor of law is granted to the faith of the party, rather than to the marriage doubtfully valid.[65]

To overthrow this presumption of law, the Church requires proof of the invalidity of the marriage. To apply this to the matter at hand, if a marriage is attacked as being invalid because of the presence in the contract of a condition contrary to the essential indissolubility of that contract, what proof does the Church require for establishing the invalidity of that marriage? The decisions of the Sacred Roman Rota seem to make this quite clear: to establish proof of invalidity the contrary condition must be *"deducta in pactum"*. Thereupon the question arises regarding what this *deductio in pactum* means.

This expression can be understood in a twofold sense. The word *pactum* can be referred to *a pact* or an agreement which the parties attach to the marriage contract. When the *pactum* is considered under this aspect, it actually serves to prove the presence of a contrary intention; it is not the contrary intention itself.[66] In the second sense, the word *pactum* can refer to *the pact,* that is the marriage contract itself. In this sense, *deductio in pactum* means that the condition enters the marriage contract, that it is made a constitutive part of that contract. When the *pactum* is considered under this aspect, the condition or intention of the party or parties is made a *conditio sine qua non,* a condition so necessary that without it the party or parties do not intend to contract at all. In this latter case, it does not matter if it is so intended by both parties, or only by one of them without the knowledge of the other. The fact that one of the contracting parties has a positive intention not to enter an indissoluble marriage is enough in this second sense of the term to make this intention or condition a constitutive part of the contract; it is a condition *"in pactum deducta."* A *pactum* in the first sense

---

[65] Canon 1127—In re dubia privilegium fidei gaudet favore iuris. Cf. Wernz-Vidal, *Ius Matrimoniale,* n. 44, p. 60.

[66] Cf. Griese, *The Marriage Contract and the Procreation of Offspring,* p. 85.

is not required to nullify the marriage contract; even the second sense of the term nullifies the contract because of a condition contrary to the substance of marriage.[67]

The will of one or of both of the parties can be expressed as a condition or as a positive intention to exclude indissolubility; in either case it will invalidate the contract if it is intended to exclude this essential element, and if this exclusion is made an essential part of the consent. On the other hand, if the will to exclude indissolubility, whether by a positive intention or with a condition, does not enter the contract and restrict the consent, the marriage is valid.[68]

This was not the interpretation of the early commentators for the expression *"deductio in pactum."* Many of them had insisted on a literal interpretation of the words of Gregory IX in the Decretals: *"Si conditiones contra substantiam coniugii inserantur, puta, si alter dicat alteri..."* and felt that this must mean that there was some mutual agreement.[69] Thus Innocent IV [70] and Panormitanus[71] held that both parties had to agree to the condition; others held that the *deductio in pactum* referred to an agreement which both parties entered into in such a way that proof of it was available in the external forum.[72]

The evidence of an added, mutual, external pact or stipulation to the marriage contract is not required for establishing the invalidity of the marriage thus entered. With reference to such an express stipulation, the pact referred to can be defined as a stipulation added to the marriage contract by the two parties thereto, whereby they come to a decision to exclude some essential element of marriage from their consent. The added pact, however, is only a means of proving the existence of the defective consent in the external forum, and, if some other means of proving the existence of such a con-

---

[67] Cf. Griese, *op. cit.*, pp. 85-86.

[68] "If neither the contrary intention nor the contrary condition enters into the contract itself to affect the essential element of consent, the marriage is valid."—Griese, *op. cit.*, p. 88.

[69] C. 7, X, *de conditionibus appositis in desponsatione vel in aliis contractibus*, IV, 5.

[70] *Commentaria*, Lib. IV, Cap. 7, p. 562.

[71] *Commentaria*, Lib. IV, Cap. 7, n. 6.

[72] Cf. Wernz, *Ius Decretalium*, Vol. IV, Tit. X, n. 297.

trary intention can be found, the evidence of such a pact is not absolutely required for a declaration of nullity.[73]

The mere fact that both parties, or even just one of them, expressed a positive intention which excluded indissolubility from the matrimonial consent is sufficient to nullify that consent and, consequently, to nullify the marriage. If this contrary condition was made the matter of a pact added expressly to the contract, that makes the proving of such a contrary intention that much easier. It would be sufficient, however, that this one essential fact be proved, namely that one of the parties intended not to contract an indissoluble union, regardless of whether he expressed that intention to the other party or not. If one party had this intention, that fact alone affects the matrimonial consent, and this invalidates the marriage *in fact*. If this can be proved sufficiently for the external forum, so that the presumption of law in favor of the validity of that marriage can be dislodged, it has for its consequence the invalidation of the marriage *in law*.

There is a further presumption, established not by the Code but by the common opinion of canonists, that in a case wherein one party has added such a condition contrary to the *bonum sacramenti*, and the other party to the marriage has opposed such a condition, it is to be presumed that the former has withdrawn the contrary condition. The marriage is then to be presumed valid, until the contrary has been proved beyond doubt.[74] Earlier canonists has asserted the same presumption for a case wherein one party added the condition and the other party kept silent.[75] Such an assertion cannot be accepted. If it is certain that one party seriously attached his

[73] Cf. Griese, *op. cit.*, p. 89.

[74] "Quod si conditionem contra substantiam posuit una pars, alia contradixit, et ita ad matrimonium ventum est, praesumitur illa recessisse a conditione, et ideo matrimonium habendum est validum, donec contrarium probetur."—Gasparri, *De Matrimonio*, II, n. 895, p. 80. Cf. also Coronata, *De Matrimonio*, n. 513, p. 700; Payen, *De Matrimonio*, II, n. 1732, p. 134; De Becker, *De Matrimonio*, p. 126, *nota* (1).

[75] "Secus vero si alter contradicat, quia tunc matrimonium est validum perinde ac si conditio non fuisset apposita. Et idem si taceat quia censetur contradicere favore matrimonii."—Fagnanus, *Commentaria*, IV, n. 3, p. 42. Cf. also Pirhing, *Ius Canonicum*, Lib. IV, Tit. V, § III, notes 1, 2, p. 65; Schmalzgrueber, *Ius Ecclesiasticum*, Lib. IV, Tit. V, n. 116, p. 436.

consent to a condition which was against indissolubility, the acceptance of that condition by the other party need not be proved for the invalidity of that marriage to eventuate.[76]

In a review of the early decisions of the Sacred Roman Rota, which were based on instructions of the Holy Office, one finds what look like contradictory statements of jurisprudence. In these statements the Holy Office and the Rota seem to insist on evidence that express conditions or mutual pacts were made, in proof of the cases of invalidity in which the alleged cause was the intention or the condition of excluding the element of indissolubility from the marriage contract.

First, in answer to a question proposed by the Bishop of Bosnia: *"An sit validum matrimonium contractum inter Catholicum et schismaticum hereticum cum intentione foedandi vel solvendi matrimonium?"*, the Holy Office, under the date of December 2, 1680, stated: *"Si ista sint deducta in pactum, seu cum ista conditione sint contracta, matrimonia sint nulla; sin aliter, sunt valida."*[77] In answer to a series of questions proposed by Capuchin missionaries in regard to the validity of the marriages of apostates, contracted in the manner of infidels, the Holy Office replied: *"Si adsit pactum dissolubilitatis, non esse matrimonium neque sacramentum; si vero non adsit, esse matrimonium et sacramentum."* [78]

A further question was proposed to the Holy Office regarding what was to be thought of a marriage entered into with the intention of one of the parties, though it was left unexpressed, that one may obtain a divorce at will. To this the Holy Office made answer in an instruction of August 19, 1857:

> Quoties in foro externo rite constet coniuges animo et voluntate solvendi vinculum contraxisse, aut cum expressa repudii conditione in pactum deducta, matrimonium est nullum. Si vero expressa illa conditio, de matrimonio pro aliquo casu dis-

---

[76] ". . . standum est pro nullitate matrimonii, si certo constet de conditione ab una parte posita, neque requiritur alterius partis acceptatio. Sufficit enim ut consensus in una parte deficiat ut matrimonium nullum sit." — Gasparri, *De Matrimonio*, II, n. 895, p. 80. Cf. also Coronata, *op. cit.*, n. 513, p. 700; Payen, *op. cit.*, II, n. 1732, p. 134; De Becker, *op. cit.*, p. 126, nota (1).

[77] *S.C.S. Off.*, 2 dec. 1680—*Fontes*, n. 755, p. 35.

[78] *Fontes*, n. 761, p. 40.

solvendo, apposita minime fuerit, et aliunde nullum praeces-
serit impedimentum, standum pro valore contractus; exceptio
enim intentionis in foro externo non admittitur nisi probetur,
et probari nequit nisi per externam declarationem.[79]

Basing their findings upon these instructions of the Holy Office,
the judges of the Rota in their decisions, such as that in the case of
a marriage between a certain Calepodius and a certain Ludmilla,
reflect the following declarations in their animadversions *in iure*:

In iure haec prae oculis habenda sunt. Primo, non quaecumque intentio etiam exterius manifestata ad foedandum vel solvendum matrimonium dici debet sufficiens ad illud irritan-
dum, sed tantum ea quae in pactum vel conditionem in celebratione matrimonii fuit deducta . . . Secundo, haec deductio
in pactum vel conditionem in foro externo non praesumitur, sed
est concludenter probanda, secus fit locus contrariae praesumptioni.[80]

Because of this seeming contradiction between the earlier decisions of the Rota and the common jurisprudence of the Rota today,
some authors say that there has been a change in Rotal jurisprudence
over the years.[81] This does not seem indicated necessarily. The Rota
is considering its decisions as reflecting a viewpoint concerned with
the external forum of the Church. Their responses are not concerned
with the speculative question but with the giving of a practical
norm which will serve in the adjudication of specific cases in the
external forum.[82] Doheny, even more simply, places the reason for

---

[79] *Fontes*, n. 945, p. 220.

[80] S.R. Rota, Nullitatis matrimonii, coram R.P.D. Iosepho Mori, die 24 iul.
1909—*Sacrae Romanae Rotae Decisiones seu Sententiae quae iuxta Legem Propriam et Constitutionem "Sapienti Concilio" Pii PP. X prodierunt, cura eiusdem
S. Tribunalis editae* (38 vols., Romae, 1912—) I (1909), Dec. XII, pp. 102-109
(hereafter cited *S.R.R. Decisiones*).

[81] Cf. Cappello, *Tractatus Canonico-Moralis De Sacramentis* (editio quarta
emendata et aucta, 3 vols. in 4, Augustae Taurinorum: Marietti, 1944), Vol. III,
Pars 2a *De Matrimonio*, n. 599, p. 43, in footnote (hereafter cited *De Matrimonio*); Chelodi, *De Matrimonio*, n. 116, p. 126, note 2.

[82] "These responses are not concerned with the speculative question at all (although their wording is quite apodictic, yet it is *presumed* the receiver realizes
the courts or Congregations look from the external forum viewpoint). The aim

the discrepancy in the variant understanding of the expression *"deductio in pactum,"* for he says: "The jurisprudence of the S.R. Rota was not changed; but the terminology employed in a few sentences, *coram Mori,* was not in accord with the Rota's usual interpretation of the phrase." [83]

The true sense in which we are to interpret the decisions and declarations of the Church as heretofore indicated was clearly indicated in a declaration of the Sacred Roman Rota in 1914. Since indissolubility belongs to the essence of marriage by positive divine law, even the Church has no power to dispense from it in a marriage contract. It is evident, therefore, that all the declarations and general instructions of the Church regarding the *bonum sacramenti* must always be understood in the sense that any marriage contract in which the parties or one of them excludes indissolubility from the contract is no marriage contract at all. It does not matter, as regards actual invalidity of such a contract, whether that act of the will which excludes the essential indissolubility is expressed as a condition or as an act of the will. It may be made the matter of an agreement or pact, or it may not; it may even be a simple intention, and it may be disclosed to the other party or not, externalized or merely retained secretly in the mind of the party so intending that exclusion. None of these matter essentially; if indissolubility is excluded by a positive act of the will of one or both of the contracting parties, the marriage contract is null.

In the external forum, on the other hand, the presumption stands that a marriage once contracted has been contracted according to law, especially since marriage enjoys a special favor in law. Therefore, the marriage will not be declared null in the external forum because of the intention of the contracting party or parties to exclude indissolubility until the existence of that intention has been proved with certainty.[84]

---

was to give a practical rule to judge concrete cases in the external forum."—Timlin, *Conditional Matrimonial Consent,* p. 258.

[83] *Canonical Procedure in Matrimonial Cases,* Vol. I, *Formal Judicial Procedure* (2. ed., Milwaukee: Bruce, 1948), p. 949, note 35.

[84] ". . . ideoque omnes declarationes vel instructiones generales ab Ecclesia circa hanc materiam variis temporibus datae, ita prorsus intelligendae sunt, ut

In fine, the *deductio in pactum,* as an external expression of the contrary condition or intention, is certainly not required for the invalidity of a contract of marriage entered into with a condition or intention contrary to indissolubility. The *deductio in pactum,* as an external expression of one of the parties or as a mutual agreement, is not absolutely required even in the external forum for proving the presence of a contrary condition or intention. The *deductio in pactum,* however, in the sense that the condition is introduced into the marriage contract as a constitutive part of the consent of one or of both of the parties, at least by the positive intention of one not to enter an indissoluble marriage, must be proved in the external forum if the presumption established in law in favor of the stability of the marriage bond is to be overthown.

The question of the positive intention is intimately connected with the question of the influence of speculative error regarding indissolubility on the validity of the marriage contract. This will receive consideration in the following article. In the light of the declarations as handed down by the Sacred Roman Rota concerning the relationship of an *error iuris* to a conditional matrimonial consent, this specification of the *deductio in pactum* will be more clearly enunciated.

ARTICLE V. SIMPLE ERROR REGARDING INDISSOLUBILITY

As has been indicated previously, a simple error regarding the indissoluble nature of marriage is not to be confused with a condition contrary to indissolubility. Since these concepts are closely connected in the practical solution of cases in the past and present jurisprudence, it seems useful to explain more fully the basis of the

qui actu quodam positivo voluntatis in matrimonii celebratione indissolublitatem excludat, contractum irritum efficiat; sive hic voluntatis actus conditio sit vel propositum, sive in pactum deducatur, sive non, sive sit etiam simplex intentio, sive alteri parti manifestata vel non, sive expressa vel tantum in mente retenta. Quoniam vero in foro externo omne factum recte factum praesumitur donec contrarium probatum sit (et praesertim matrimonium, quod speciali gaudet favore iuris), patet quod in foro externo nequeat declarari nullum, propter voluntatem in contrahentibus Sacramenti bono contrariam, nisi haec certa sit et probata."— S.R. Rota, Parisien. — *Nullitatis matrimonii* (Goguel-Gravier), coram R.P.D. Frederico Cattani, die 17 apr. 1915—*AAS,* VII (1915), p. 452.

juridical distinction between the two. Many of the marriage cases presented for adjudication in the Church's tribunals today are based on the assertion of one or both of the parties that the marriage was entered into with the idea that, should the bond prove onerous, it could be ended by divorce. Will this error regarding the indissoluble nature of marriage be equivalent to a condition contrary to an indissoluble bond?

In the consideration of this problem, one may study it from the aspect of the jurisprudence of the Church. From this it is clear that such an error, if it is a simple error, will not invalidate the marriage. If, however, this error is incorporated as a condition into the contract, it will be a condition contrary to the essential indissolubility of that contract, and the marriage will be invalid. One may also study this problem from the viewpoint of a philosophical explanation of simple error to see if a distinction between such an error and conditional consent can be maintained in the face of the philosophical axiom: *Nil volitum nisi praecognitum.*

A. The Jurisprudence of the Church

This problem is not a new one; it was raised long ago by the marriage formula in use among the Protestant sects, specifically among the Calvinists. The teaching of the canonists was admirably forwarded by the treatment which Pope Benedict XIV accorded to the problem in his work *De Synodo Diocesana.*

Benedict began by giving the source of the problem, the formulary in the Calvinist ritual of marriage:

> Dic vir: Verus Deus, qui est Pater et Filius et Spiritus, et perfecta Sancta Trinitas, unus vere aeternus Deus, ita te adiuvet in tua vera fide quoad personam, quam manu tenes, amas, ex amore illam accipis in perpetuam uxorem, illa contentaberis, cum illa patieris, nec illam tua et illius vita durante, nec in sanitate, nec in infirmitate, nec in infelici statu, nec in illa illius aerumna deseres, *quoadusque in sua honestate et puritate permanserit.* Ita te Deus adiuvit.[85]

---

[85]Benedictus XIV, *De Synodo Dioecesana,* Lib. XIII, Cap. XXII, n. 1, p. 289.

A Calvinist woman had married a Calvinist man in Transylvania [86] according to this formula. Later she became a Catholic, and then, while her first husband was still alive, she entered a marriage with a Catholic. Discussing the validity of this marriage, Benedict taught that a marriage between Calvinists was certainly a valid one, even though they labored, as did their coreligionists, under the false notion that the marriage bond could be dissolved because of adultery. The reason for this was that they contracted with the general intention of entering a valid marriage according to the will of Christ, a marriage which is indissoluble. Their private error did not affect their general intention, on which the perpetuity and the validity of the marriage contract depended. Consequently, this woman's second marriage was declared null and void.[87]

In his reasoning Pope Benedict made a strong distinction between a true condition against indissolubility and a simple error about this quality. Even though the contracting parties married under the mistaken notion that marriage could be dissolved because of adultery, the marriage is valid, as long as the parties were not led by this error to make their contract dependent on this condition that the marriage would be dissolved if one of them committed adultery. Such a condition attached to the matrimonial consent would, of course, invalidate the contract, since the consent is thereby vitiated. The contracting parties, if they truly will the contract, must will the substance of that contract; if, therefore, they add to that contract something which is evidently incompatible with its substance, they are, in effect, refusing to consent to the contract. Without the consent of the contracting parties, as is evident, there can be no marriage.[88]

Despite their erroneous concepts about the nature of marriage,

---

[86] This was formerly part of Hungary, in what is now the central part of Rumania.

[87] Benedictus XIV, *ibidem*, n. III, p. 290.

[88] ". . . quicumque contractum vult, necesse est, ut eiusdem substantiam velit; ideoque, si contrahentes, in matrimonii foedere ineundo, conditionem apponunt illius substantiae contrariam, certissimum hoc est argumentum, nequaquam eos in veri matrimonii contractum consentire; sine contrahentium autem consensu, matrimonium esse non potest."—Benedictus XIV, *ibid.*, n. VII, p. 293.

however, the parties contract a valid union as long as they do not add any condition based on that error. The reason for this is that the speculative error which does not lead to a positive act of the will contrary to the substance of marriage is absorbed by the general intention of the parties to enter a true marriage, as Christ instituted it, that is, a *perpetual union*.[89]

As Benedict pointed out, this presumption had to give way to any full proof of the contrary, so that any express condition to end the marriage in case of adultery, as a particular intention of the contracting party, would not be absorbed by the general intention of doing what Christ willed. This particular intention against the essential note of indissolubility would invalidate the contract.[90]

Adverting to two marriages which had been declared invalid after being contracted according to the Calvinist ritual, Benedict noted that in both there was more than mere concomitant error; there was annexed to the consent a condition which was contrary to the indissoluble nature of marriage and thus nullified the contract.[91]

In the nineteenth century there were several instructions of the

---

[89] "Quod si expressa illa conditio . . . apposita minime fuerit, quantumvis contrahentes in eo fuerint errore . . . locus est praesumptioni, ut dum matrimonium, prout a Christo institutum fuit, inire voluerunt, illud omnino perpetuum, ac, interveniente etiam adulterio, insolubile contrahere voluerint; praevalente nimirum generali, quam diximus, voluntate de matrimonio iuxta Christi institutionem ineundo, atque privatum illum errorem quodammodo absorbente, quo fit, ut matrimonium ita contractum, validum firmumque maneat."—Benedictus XIV, *loc. cit.*

[90] "At, ubi contrahentes in ipso matrimonii contractu expressam apposuerunt conditionem de dissolvendo quoad vinculum matrimonio in casu adulterii; iam fieri nequit, ut error particularis absorptus maneat a generali voluntate contrahendi matrimonium, prout a Christo Domino institutum fuit; sed potius voluntas generalis eiusmodi extinguitur et suffocatur ab errore particulari, qui manifeste praevalet ac dominatur; atqui hinc oritur nullitas matrimonii, in quo contrahendo apposita fuit conditio ipsius substantiae contraria."—Benedictus XIV, *ibid.,* pp. 293-294.

[91] ". . . valida vere censenda esse matrimonia, ab iis contracta, qui licet falso sibi persuadeant, adulterio interveniente, matrimonii vinculum solvendum esse, id ipsum tamen nullo modo in pactum conditionemque deducunt; at irrita et nulla esse connubia in quibus id expresse consulto fuerit tamquam pactum atque conditio."—Benedictus XIV, *ibid.,* n. IX, p. 295.

Holy Office which stressed the distinction between an antecedent error which leads to the addition of a condition contrary to indissolubility and a merely concomitant error which has no effect on the consent nor on the validity of the contract. Under the date of July 22, 1840, the Holy Office answered questions proposed as a result of a declaration of nullity by the General Congregation of the Holy Office on May 20, 1754 in the case of a marriage contracted before a Calvinist minister. It was asked: "What if two Catholics were thus married, but, despite the formula used, declared that they intended in good faith to contract according to the mind of the Church?" Secondly: "What if this was a mixed marriage, and the Catholic so intended to enter the contract according to the mind of the Church?" The Holy Office replied:

Matrimonium inter duos Catholicos qui in sensu Ecclesiae contrahunt, interveniente declaratione contrahentium, esse validum et indissolubile.

Matrimonium mixtum esse nullum, scilicet parte acatholica expresse declarante se contrahere matrimonium de praesenti iuxta formulam perpetuitati matrimonii contrariam. Quod si pars Catholica expresse declaret se intendere contrahere in sensu Ecclesiae et pars heretica ei assentiatur, adhuc validum haberi debet.[92]

This the instruction indicates: 1) the declaration of intention of the two Catholic parties withstands the normally invalidating effect of the contrary condition in the formula; 2) the express intention of the one party who places a contrary condition prevails over the intention of the other, and the contract is null; 3) the express intention of the Catholic party, accepted by the heretic, prevails over the otherwise invalidating condition.

A second instruction of the Holy Office on April 6, 1843 indicated that there were in use among the Protestant sects several formularies in which a condition contrary to indissolubility appeared in express words, and there were many more rites among them in which such a condition was indicated by circumstances. The latter would be true in regions where the rite, if used in the common

---

[92] *Collectanea S. C. de Prop. Fidei*, Vol. I, n. 903, *S.C.S. Off.*, (Promont. Bonae Spei), 22 iul. 1840—*Fontes*, n. 883.

manner, evidenced the fact that there was no consent to an indissoluble bond. Nevertheless, the instruction pointed out, it was not to be doubted that there could be a valid marriage in any case wherein there was just a concomitant error regarding the indissoluble bond, since the general will of the contracting parties to contract marriage according to the mind of Christ absorbed this private error. Whenever the formula used expressed a contrary condition explicitly or implicitly, however, this so-called general will was dislodged by a particular intention, and the marriage thus contracted was invalid. The indications that may point to the presence of a condition against indissolubility the Holy Office found in the ceremonies of the marriage, in the words used in the formulary for the expression of the consent, etc. Whenever these circumstances indicate the presence of a condition against this substantial element, the contract is null. For this reason, if two baptized persons entered a marriage contract before a Protestant minister or a civil magistrate and declared that they entered that contract according to the laws or customs of that region, their marriage would be invalid.[93]

---

[93] "Certum est matrimonium contractum cum conditione ipsius substantiae, et nominatim ipsius indissolubilitati repugnante, nullum esse. Iam vero non paucae, formulae a protestantibus adhibitae illa conditione irritante contaminatae sunt, in quibus expressis verbis inhaeret haec conditio: *contraho tecum donec in fidelitate permanseris;* immo etiam voluntas aliquando, satis aperte factis exprimitur, vel verbis simul et factis, dum verba vel facta interpretantur ipse usus et consuetudo illorum locorum, ita ut abfuisse intelligatur consensus in contractum perpetuum et indissolubilem.

Tametsi autem dubitandum non sit, quin validum matrimonium contrahi possit cum errore mere concomitante circa eius indissolubilitatem, quia tunc praevalet generalis voluntas contrahendi matrimonium iuxta institutionem Christi, et generalis illa voluntas privatum errorem quodammodo absorbet, attamen ubi adhibetur formula cum explicita vel implicita illa conditione, iam fieri nequit, ut particularis error absorptus maneat a generali voluntate contrahendi iuxta institutionem Christi . . .

Circa alias formulas ita pariter statuendum, si vel implicite, vel explicite conditionem contineant matrimonii substantiae repugnantem . . . Ex hisce omnibus, et etiam ex adiunctis loci circumstantiis, ab eo qui in iis praesens sit facile dignosci poterit quaenam sit prava coniugum intentio.

Quia vero contingere posset, ut duo baptizati (de his enim nunc agitur) contraherent coram ministro protestantico vel coram Principe, declarando se contrahere iuxta leges, vel consuetudinem regionis, ubi etiam levibus ex causis dissolvi

According to an instruction of Dec. 11, 1850, the Holy Office forbade missionaries, in the capacity of civil officials, to assist at the marriages of non-Catholics of their territory who married according to the custom of that territory, which admitted divorce and remarriage.[94]

A further case was proposed in an instruction of Aug. 19, 1857, regarding a Tahitian woman who entered a marriage according to the law of her region which admitted divorce, intending to use this if circumstances should later demand it. Having abandoned her husband, she entered a second and a third union, but then desired to become a Catholic, although she could not return to her first husband who had since remarried, and she did not herself want to remain unmarried. The question was then proposed: What was to be thought of such a marriage, entered into with an unexpressed intention that the marriage might later be dissolved? Could such a person be left in good faith, getting a renewal of her consent to the present marriage and blessing it? The Holy Office responded:

> Quoties in foro externo rite constet coniuges animo et voluntate solvendi vinculum contraxisse, aut cum expressa repudii conditione in pactum deducta, matrimonium est nullum. Si vero expressa illa conditio de matrimonio pro aliquo casu dissolvendo, apposita minime fuerit, et aliunde nullum praecesserit impedimentum, standum pro valore contractus; exceptio enim intentionis in foro externo non admittitur nisi probetur, et probari nequit nisi per externam declarationem.[95]

It is evident, then, that the marriage of a pagan or of a heretic is not to be presumed invalid in view of any attached condition contrary to indissolubility, even though the parties involved may share in the common error of their region that marriage is dissoluble at the will of the parties or for certain specific causes. In each case one is to study the intention of the contracting parties in order to discover whether just a simple concomitant error was in their mind,

---

solent, talia matrimonia irrita essent."—*S.C.S. Off., instr.* (*ad Vic. Ap. Oceaniae*), 6 apr. 1843—*Fontes*, n. 894, pp. 171-172.

[94] *S.C.S. Off.* (*Vic. Ap. Sandwic.*), 11 dec. 1850, ad 27—*Collectanea S.C. de Prop. Fidei*, Vol. I, n. 1054—*Fontes*, n. 913.

[95] *S.C.S. Off.* (Tahiti), 19 aug. 1857, ad 1—*Fontes*, n. 945; *Collectanea S.C. de Prop. Fidei*, Vol. I, n. 1147.

or whether this error led to the affixing of their consent to a condition or a pact against the stability of the marriage bond. This was
even more clearly indicated by instructions of the Holy Office to
the Vicar Apostolic of Central Oceania and to the Bishop of Nes-
qually. These instructions emphasized that only those marriages
were to be considered invalid which were contracted under such
formulas or rites which incorporated the dissolubility of the marriage bond in the form of a pact or condition added to the contract.
If, however, there existed merely an error about the indissoluble
nature of marriage, which did not affect the contract, the marriage
was to be considered valid. The missionaries of the regions to which
the instructions were sent no longer were to consider all pagan or
heretical marriages invalid *a priori* in view of an attached condition
against indissolubility.[96]

The jurisprudence of the Sacred Roman Rota has always followed
this same doctrine in the adjudication of marriages in which the
validity was impugned in view of an erroneous belief of the parties
that their marriage could be dissolved *quoad vinculum*. Thus, in the
case of a marriage so impugned, the Rota on July 24, 1909, gave
the decision: *non constare de nullitate matrimonii*. In its decision
the Rota observed that only that intention which was *in pactum vel
conditionem deducta* would be deemed sufficient to nullify the matrimonial contract and, furthermore, that *deductio* had to be proved
by conclusive arguments. Only in such a case could the general intention of contracting marriage according to the law of Christ be

[96]*S.C.S. Off., instr.* (Ad Vic. Ap. Oceaneae Centralis), 18 dec. 1872: "Errorem
menti inhaerentem, qui tamen non sit deductus in pactum sive conditionem, valid-
itati matrimonii non officere, eoque tantum in casu invalidum reddere, cum,
consideratis formulis, quae in actu contractus adhibitae sunt, merito dici possit
fuisse in pactum deductum . . . Illa matrimonia invalida sunt . . . quae contracta fuerint sub illis formulis vel fortasse aliis eiusdem valoris, in quibus scilicet
deducta fuerit in pactum sive conditionem matrimonii dissolubilitas . . . In cete-
ris enim matrimoniis, in quibus error de matrimonii dissolubilitate nullo modo
fuit in pactum deductus . . . omnino valida haberi debeant."—*Collectanea S.C.
de Prop. Fidei*, Vol. II, n. 1392; *Fontes*, n. 1024, S.C.S., *Off., instr.* (ad Ep. Nes-
quallien.), 24 ian. 1877: "Quamvis autem certum sit conditionem contrariam
perpetuitati et indissolubilitati coniugalis vinculi ipsum matrimonium omnino
nullum atque irritum reddere; tamen ad hoc oportet ut talis conditio aliquo
modo a contrahentibus in pactum fuerit deducta."—*Fontes*, n. 1050.

absorbed and destroyed by the contrary will of the contracting parties.[97]

The final decision of the Rota in the famous Castellane-Gould case,[98] given on February 8, 1915, was: *non constare de nullitate matrimonii.* The basis for the decision was this same distinction the Rota drew between a speculative error (*error iuris*) and a condition contrary to the sacramental stability of the bond of marriage. Ignorance and error are found in the operations of the intellect; it is by an act of the will, however, that a marriage contract is effected. The state of the intellect, therefore, regarding the essential nature of marriage, namely whether the intellect is in error about indissolubility or not, will not affect the validity of the marriage contract unless the speculative error in the intellect about the perpetuity of the marriage leads one or both of the contracting parties to make a positive act of the will excluding an indissoluble bond.[99]

[97] "Si coniuges cognoscentes quidem legem permittentem matrimonii solubilitatem ob compartis adulterium, cum hac positiva intentione matrimonium inierunt . . . profecto tunc matrimonium dici debet nullum, cum haec positiva intentio destruat matrimonium ob defectum animi matrimonialis in suum verum obiectum, seu matrimonium indissolubile; seu aliis verbis, intentio generalis contrahendi matrimonium iuxta legem Christi absorbetur et destruitur a contraria voluntate contrahentium." — S.R. Rota, Nullitatis matrimonii, coram R.P.D. Iosepho Mori, die 24 iul. 1909—*R.R.R. Decisiones*, I (1909), Dec. XII, n. 5, pp. 102-109.

[98] This was the case in which the marriage of the Count Boni de Castellane, a Catholic, to Anna Gould, an Episcopalian of great wealth and social position in New York, was impugned by the Count on the grounds that Anna Gould had placed a condition contrary to the indissoluble bond of marriage before the marriage took place.

[99] "Si quis ergo matrimonium dissolubile contrahere vellet, illud vellet quale consistere nequit et proinde vellet absurdum. Diximus: *si quis vellet,* non autem si quis nesciret indissolubilitatem esse matrimonio essentialem . . . Ignorantia enim et error afficiunt intellectum dum e contra . . matrimonium perficitur voluntate.

Ullimode ergo consistere nequit matrimonium simul cum voluntate, vel etiam unius contrahentis, positive contraria illius indissolubilitati, quia in eo deesset consensus, seu esset fictitius tantum et simulatus. Et hoc verum est, quocumque modo haec voluntas exprimatur."—*S.R.R. Decisiones,* Vol. V (1913), Dec. XVI. n. 17, pp. 190-191. This case was adjudicated by the Rota in all three instances. The first decision was: *non constare de nullitate* (Dec. 9, 1911); cf. *AAS,* IV (1912), 146-156. In the second instance the decision was: *sententiam Rotalem*

From this consideration of the jurisprudence as practiced by the Holy Office and the Roman Rota, one can see that the distinction between a simple error and a condition contrary to the indissoluble bond of marriage must be upheld. The criterion of judgement is this: if the error about indissolubility is a simple error, which remains in the intellect and does not affect the consent of the will, the marriage is valid. If, however, the intellectual error leads to the affixing of a pact or a condition against the indissoluble element of the marriage bond, it is *not* a simple error, but a condition properly so called, and the marriage, because of this condition, is null. The assertion of one or both of the parties that such an error of the intellect led to a contrary intention, actually and not only interpretatively present in the contracting, is not to be accepted *ipso facto;* the presence of such an intention is to be proved conclusively in the external forum. One must still keep in mind, of course, that in the forum of conscience a marriage is or is not valid objectively in so far as such an intention, contrary to the essential element of indissolubility in the marriage bond, is or is not present in the will of one or both of the contracting parties.

B. PHILOSOPHICAL EXPLANATION OF THIS DISTINCTION

Canon 1084 declares that a simple error regarding the attribute of indissolubility, even though it is the cause of the contract, does not vitiate the marriage. Yet there is the accepted philosophical axiom that the will cannot act except upon presentation by the intellect of the object willed: *"nil volitum nisi praecognitum."* How can these two elements be reconciled in harmony with the canonical jurisprudence? The Castellane-Gould case, cited above, may serve as an illustration of the difficulty. It was clear in this case that there was a theoretical error regarding the indissoluble nature of the marriage bond, and that this error led to the making of the contract. Miss Gould was a non-Catholic and believed in the possibility of a divorce *quoad vinculum;* she entered the marriage the more readily because she did believe that, should the marriage prove unhappy,

---

diei 9 decembris 1911 esse infirmandam in casu (March 1, 1913); cf. *AAS*, V (1913), 312-332. The final decision confirmed the sentence of the first instance: *non constare de nullitate* (Feb. 8, 1915); cf. *AAS*, VII (1915), 292-313.

she could divorce her husband and contract a further marriage. She was thus in error about the essential note of indissolubility in marriage. Because of this error her intellect presented marriage as a dissoluble union; how, then, could her will be said not to have excluded this note of indissolubility from her consent? Was her intellectual error not equivalent to an intention or condition contrary to the substance of marriage?

The principle is clear from juridical procedure, but is this procedure philosophically and psychologically possible? In an individual case the *facts* may be difficult to ascertain with a view to discerning whether this specific case deals with a simple error or with a true condition, but when it is clearly understood, the principle of law involved is indeed valid.

To understand the principle, the definition of simple error must be clearly understood first of all. *"Simplex dicitur error, quousque quis, etsi theoretice erroneas teneat doctrinas de proprietatibus matrimonii, positivo tamen actu voluntatis nullam ex eis excludit."* [100] Thus a simple error is a false judgement of the intellect regarding the indissoluble nature of marriage, which judgement, however, remains in the intellect and does not modify the consent of the will to a contract of marriage.

It might be objected that the intellect in a case of simple error conceives marriage as a dissoluble union. If, then, the will acts upon its object *as presented by the intellect,* and the intellect conceives that object as dissoluble, the will must will marriage as a dissoluble union.

In answer to this, we explain the axiom: *nil volitum nisi praecognitum* as follows. It is true that the will cannot act upon an object which is *completely* unknown to the intellect, but it does not follow from this that the intellect must know every facet of the object. The will follows the representation of the object as made by the intellect, unless there is an actual intention to the contrary which prevails. This is evident from the possibility that a Catholic who understands clearly the indissoluble nature of marriage can, nevertheless, exclude this note of indissolubility in his attempt to contract a dissoluble marriage. Here an actual prevailing intention

[100] Sipos, *Enchiridion Iuris Canonici,* § 130, p. 499.

of the will overrides the presentation which the intellect offered to the will.

There can be an error which leads to the making of a condition contrary to indissolubility by the will, because the will embraces the erroneous concept of the intellect and incorporates it in its consent to the contract. In this case the marriage is invalid. There can also be an error which remains in the intellect and does not affect the consent of the will, because of a prevailing actual intention of the will which is contrary to the exclusion of indissolubility in the marriage contract. In this case the marriage contract is valid.

In the case of speculative error it will be necessary to judge in this apparent conflict of intentions which intention prevails. As the problem is proposed, there is a general intention of entering marriage, which is indissoluble by its nature; the intention to enter a dissoluble union is only interpretative, in that *one would have* made an actual intention of entering a dissoluble marriage *if* one had been asked about it, or *if* one had thought such a specification necessary. Such an intention is no intention at all; it is a supposition of what would have been done. Such a supposition or hypothetical intention certainly cannot prevail over the general intention of entering marriage, which is expressed in the act of consent, which directly derives from the will.

If there is an actual intention to enter a dissoluble union, this intention will prevail over the general intention. In this case there is no longer just a simple error, but there is, rather, a specific contrary intention or condition with reference to the essential element of sacramental indissolubility. It will be the duty of the adjucating tribunal to decide in individual instances whether there is such a prevailing actual intention not to enter an indissoluble marriage, or whether there is just a speculative error of the intellect along with the general intention of entering marriage according to its institution, so that this general intention prevails over the concomitant error. Because of the favor which marriage enjoys in law, the presumption will be that no such actual contrary intention was elicited; positive proof will have to be adduced to the contrary in order to overthrow this presumption. Even though this error was the cause of the contract in that the parties would not have entered the contract if they had known that the marriage bond was indissoluble, the will, by supposition, gave actual consent to marriage as it is, and this actual consent must prevail over what might have been intended in some hypothesis.[101]

ARTICLE VI. TRUE INVALIDATING CONDITIONS AGAINST INDISSOLUBILITY

Through the progress of this study the specific object of conditions contrary to the essential note of indissolubility in the marriage contract was introduced by a process of exclusion. For this reason, the doctrine regarding such conditions has already been explained in the course of presentation. It seems apropos at this point, however, to sum up this doctrine in an organized form.

Canon 1092 indicates in section two the invalidating effect of such a condition:

> Conditio semel apposita et non revocata, si [sit] de futuro contra matrimonii substantiam, illud reddit invalidum.

This invalidating law deserves a closer examination.

Conditio

A condition, as here understood, is some circumstance attached to the matrimonial consent, so that the validity of the consent of the one who sets or invokes the condition depends on the fulfillment or verification of this condition. If such a condition refers to the indissolubility of the marriage bond, the attaching of such a condition to the marriage contract will invalidate that contract. Thus, any true condition against indissolubility nullifies the contract.[102] It does not matter whether this condition is suspensive or resolvent.[103] Even immoral or impossible conditions against indissolubility will invalidate a marriage contract if they are seriously

---

[101] Further discussion of this solution may be found in Bouscaren-Ellis, *Canon Law*, pp. 558-560; Timlin, *Conditional Matrimonial Consent*, pp. 260-283.

[102] Cf. Sanchez, *De Matrimonii Sacramento*, Lib. I, Disp. IX, n. 3, p. 314; Navarrus, *De Matrimonii Impedimentis*, Cap. XXII, n. 62, p. 369; *Schmalzgrueber, Ius Ecclesiasticum*, Lib. IV, Tit. V, n. 115, p. 435.

[103] Cf. Fagnanus, *Commentaria*, Lib. IV, nn. 6-7, p. 42; Sanchez, *op. cit.*, n. 2, p. 314.

attached to it.[104] Honorable and worthy conditions against the indissolubility will also invalidate the marriage.[105]

A condition must, however, be distinguished from other additions or specifications collateral with the consent, such as modes, causes, demonstrations and time clauses.[106]

Semel apposita

The attaching of the condition must be such that the condition is incorporated in the contract if it is to affect the consent in such a manner as to make it a conditional consent. To invalidate the marriage contract, this condition need not be placed by way of mutual agreement on the side of both parties, nor need it be in the form of a specific stipulation added to the contract. It must be *"deducta in pactum"* if external proof is to avail, in the sense namely that it exists by a mutual agreement, or was a *conditio sine qua non* added by one of the parties. In the internal forum of conscience, however, any condition against the indissoluble nature of marriage will invalidate it, regardless of how this internal intention is expressed, whether with a condition or with a simple intention or resolution, and whether in or apart from the form of a pact. It may be intended expressly or tacitly, explicitly or implicitly, by one or by both of the parties to the contract, as long as it does affect the consent.[107]

Non revocata

Naturally, if the condition contrary to indissolubility was placed before the sealing of the contract, and the parties or the party who added it revoked such a condition before the actual contracting, it no longer has any effect on the consent, and the marriage is valid. This revocation can be made explicitly in words or in writing, or the party who made it may revoke his contrary condition implicitly by showing his or her contrary will.[108] The common can-

---

[104] Cf. Sanchez, *op. cit.*, Lib. V, Disp. IV, n. 19, p. 303; De Lugo, *De Iustitia et Iure*, Vol. II, Disp. XXII, Sec. XIII, n. 340 and n. 342, p. 53; Reiffenstuel, *Ius Canonicum Universum*, Lib. IV, Tit. V, n. 3, p. 428.

[105] Cf. Soto, *Commentarium*, Vol. II, Dist. 29, Q. II, Art. III, p. 189.

[106] Cf. *supra*, pp. 79-80.

[107] Cf. *Fontes*, n. 1024; *Fontes*, n. 1050; *S.R.R. Decisiones*, I (1909), Dec. XII, pp. 102-109.

[108] Cf. Timlin, *Conditional Matrimonial Consent*, pp. 195-197.

onical commentary contends that one presumably has revoked his contrary condition if he proceeds with the contract after the other party to the contract has shown opposition to such a condition. This is, of course, only a presumption, and hence must give way to the proof of the contrary.[109] The same presumption does not hold, according to the better opinion, if one party has placed the condition against perpetuity and the other merely remains silent.[110]

If the contrary condition was affixed by mutual consent, it will not suffice that one party revokes the condition. Marriage is effected by a mutual consent; if the consent of one party is still deficient, there can be no matrimonial contract.[111]

De futuro

A condition can look to the past, the present or the future, in as much as the circumstance from which the validity and the obligation consequent on the matrimonial consent is made to depend exists in the past, the present or the future. Only a condition that has to reckon with the future, however, can be truly invalidating, since properly there can be no condition if it does not look to the future.[112] There can be a condition *de futuro* which takes the grammatical form of a condition *de praesenti,* such as: I marry you, if we now contract for two years. Such a condition does not actually look to the present, but it looks forward into the future for an event that will be verified after two years.[113] A condition that looks to the present or to the past is not properly a condition. If unverified it precludes the emergence of any obligation at all, and if verified the existing or the consequent obligation arises apart from any reference to it.[114] Only a future contingency can be set as a condition in the proper sense, because only such a condition actually

---

[109] Cf. Gasparri, *De Matrimonio,* II, n. 895, p. 80; Coronata, *De Matrimonio,* n. 513, p. 700; Payen, *De Matrimonio,* II, n. 1732, p. 134.

[110] Cf. Gasparri, *op. cit.,* II, n. 895, p. 80; Coronata, *op. cit.,* n. 513, p. 700; Payen, *op. cit.,* II, n. 1732, p. 134.

[111] Cf. canon 1081, § 1.

[112] Cf. Sanchez, *op. cit.,* Lib. V, Disp. IX, n. 2, p. 314.

[113] Cf. Sanchez, *loc. cit.*

[114] Cf. Pirhing, *Ius Canonicum,* Lib. IV, Tit. V, § 1, n. I, p. 63.

suspends the consent, and this, by definition, belongs to the nature of a condition.[115]

Contra matrimonii substantiam

A condition may be contrary to the substance of marriage in that it excludes the essential object of the contract, the *"ius in corpus, perpetuum et exclusivum, in ordine ad actus per se aptos ad prolis generationem,"* [116] or either of its essential properties, the *"unitas ac indissolubilitas, quae in matrimonio christiano peculiarem obtinent firmitatem ratione sacramenti."* [117] Following the terminology of St. Augustine,[118] authors therefore distinguished conditions against the substance of marriage as conditions *contra bonum prolis* (exclusion of the *ius coniugale,* or the exclusion of children), *contra bonum fidei* (exclusion of the essential unity or fidelity in marriage) and *contra bonum sacramenti* (exclusion of the essential indissolubility of marriage). In reference to the last named *bonum,* it is not possible to invoke a distinction or to differentiate between the exclusion of the very obligation inherent in the indissolubility of marriage and the exclusion of the fulfillment of that obligation. Both the obligation and the execution of this blessing of marriage belong essentially to the contract of marriage. Any condition contrary to even the fulfillment of this obligation nullifies the contract, since it abstracts from the very substance of marriage. In such a case there can be no true marital consent; it is vitiated at its very source. There can be no true marriage if its bond is not inseparable; whoever wills a true marriage must will that it be indissoluble. If one wills a dissoluble union, one does not will marriage at all.[119]

With reference to any condition contrary to indissolubility, one must always distinguish it from a simple error of the intellect which judges falsely that marriage can be dissolved at will by the parties,

---

[115] Cf. Coronata, *De Matrimonio,* n. 493, p. 670. Other conditions are conditions in the wide sense only. Cf. *supra,* pp. 79 and 84.

[116] Canon 1081, § 2.

[117] Canon 1013, § 2.

[118] *De Genesi ad Litteram,* Lib. IX, Cap. 7, n. 12, *CSEL,* XXXXVIII, 275-276.

[119] Cf. Sanchez, *op. cit.,* Lib. II, Disp. XXIX, n. 12, p. 116; Coronata, *op. cit.,* n. 465, p. 626; Chelodi, *De Matrimonio,* n. 117, p. 142; Wernz-Vidal, *Ius Matrimoniale,* n. 462, pp. 595-596.

or for specific causes. Because of this distinction between a simple error and a contrary condition, a marriage entered into with the condition, attached by at least one of the parties thereto, that in case of unhappiness or adultery the union will be dissolved, is invalid; a marriage entered into with, or even because of this false notion of the nature of marriage will be valid, provided that this notion remains in the intellect and is not made into a condition by an act of the will.[120]

Illud reddit invalidum

This has been the constant tradition of the Church, as is evident from the historical synopsis of this study. The reason for the invalidity is evident. Consent makes the marriage contract; this is so necessarily an act of the parties to the contract that no human power can supply it, if it is lacking.[121] Since this is so, when that consent is lacking the attempted contract is null; the marriage is invalid. The traditional and evident reason for the invalidity of a conditional matrimonial consent, which makes the marital consent dependent on a condition which is contrary to the indissoluble nature of marriage, is this: nothing can subsist without its substance. The substance of marriage consists in the consent to a conjugal union, in which consent there must necessarily be consent to an indissoluble union, since indissolubility is essential to a true marriage. Therefore, any condition which is opposed to the essential perpetuity of marriage eradicates the very substance of marriage and consequently nullifies that marriage. This invalidity derives from the requirements of the natural law itself, not from the positive legislation of the Church.[122]

Here again one must recall the essential notion that the invalidity of the marriage, when it is contracted with a condition contrary to indissolubility, does not depend fundamentally (*in se*) on any proof of the presence of a contrary intention or condition, nor does it

---

[120] Cf. *supra*, pp. 127-130.

[121] Canon 1081, § 1.

[122] Cf. Sanchez, *op. cit.*, Lib. V, Disp. IX, n. 2, p. 314; Navarrus, *De Matrimonii Impedimentis*, Cap. XXII, n. 62, p. 369; Soto, *Commentarium*, Dist. 29, Q. II, Art. III, p. 189; De Lugo, *De Iustitia et Iure*, Vol. II, Disp. XXII, Sec. XIII, n. 348, p. 54.

depend on any declaration of nullity implemented by the ecclesiastical authorities. The marriage is valid or invalid, depending on whether there was, in reality, a contrary intention or condition affixed to the consent given by one or both of the parties to that contract. For the obtaining of proof in the external forum, for the permission to enter another and a valid union, for a juridical basis on which to declare the putative marriage null and void, external proof of such an intention or condition is indeed required. This is, however, just a *declaration* of invalidity; the invalidity itself is the result of the existence of such a condition against the sacramental stability. Even though there may be no evidence of it, the mere fact that one of the parties had a positive intention to exclude an indissoluble marriage is, of itself, sufficient for the emergence of an invalid marriage.[123]

This, then, is a summation of the doctrine on conditions which invalidate the matrimonial contract because of an exclusion of the *bonum sacramenti,* the essential indissolubility of a conjugal union. There remains only a consideration of the modes, causes, demonstrations and time clauses, and the determination of their effect on the validity or invalidity of the juridical act of matrimonial consent. By way of contrast and comparison, with this determination, the full nature of the invalidating contrary condition will be evident.

ARTICLE VII. THE EFFECT OF OTHER MODIFICATIONS OF THE CONSENT

A. TIME CLAUSES

A time clause added to the matrimonial consent is the application of a *terminus a quo* or of a *terminus ad quem* to the contract of marriage. This terminus, called *dies* by many authors, may be certain or uncertain, depending on whether the particular time when the *dies* will occur is certain or uncertain. There is common agreement on this matter. If the time clause is added as a *terminus a quo,* either certain ("I contract with you from Easter Sunday on") or uncertain ("I contract with you when I am discharged from military service"), it has the juridical effect of a suspensive condition, and

---

[123] S.R. Rota, Parisien., Nullitatis matrimonii (Goguel-Gravier), coram R.P.D. Friderico Cattoni, die 17 apr. 1915—*AAS,* VII (1915), 452.

it will effect a valid marriage when the condition is fulfilled. If, however, the time clause is added as a *terminus ad quem,* whether certain or uncertain, to indicate a time when the marriage bond would cease, such as: "I contract with you for three years" or "until I find one more worthy" the time clause has the effect of a resolvent condition, and, for the reason that it militates against the essential indissolubility of marriage, it also invalidates the contract.[124]

B. Causes and Demonstrations

A cause added to the marriage consent, as was indicated previously,[125] is the expression of the reason because of which the party entered the contract. A demonstration is the indication of some quality which the party knows to exist or thinks to exist in the other party to the contract. Although Navarrus had held that such a cause or demonstration would invalidate the union if it militated against the substance of marriage,[126] authors are in common agreement to the contrary, namely that these factors neither invalidate the contract nor suspend the consent. Sanchez and most of the authors taught that inherently (*per se*) such factors as causes and demonstrations, whether immoral or contrary to the substance, whether true or false, are always to be held as not added at all; the marriage is valid. Sanchez adduced as reason for this view the fact that a false demonstration could not invalidate a legacy, which enjoys less favor in law than marriage. Secondly, to nullify a marriage the nullifying agent must refer to the substance of the contract or to its essential nature; a cause or a demonstration, however, does not refer to the substance, or to the essential nature of marriage, but to an opinion in the mind of the contracting party, or to motives which induce him to consent. Thirdly, demonstrations and causes are neither total

---

[124] Cf. F. Schmier, *Jurisprudentia,* II, Lib. IV, Tract. II, Cap. II, Sec. III, § III, n. 142, p. 397; De Angelis, *Praelectiones Iuris Canonici* (5 vols., Romae, Parisiis, 1877-1891), Lib. IV, Tit. V. n. 7, p. 155 (hereafter cited *Praelectiones*); Wernz, *Ius Decretalium,* IV, Tit. X, Scholion II, p. 451.

[125] Cf. *supra,* p. 80.

[126] "Et quamvis haec tria, scilicet causa, modus et demonstratio nunquam suspendant, annihilant tamen quando sunt contra substantiam aut bonum matrimonii."—Navarrus, *De Matrimonii Impedimentis,* Cap. XXII, n. 62, p. 370.

nor partial objects of the contract, for they are simply postulated as antecedent to it. Therefore, these cannot nullify the contract.[127]

C. Modes

The mode, which is an intent or agreement running collaterally with the contract, is an obligation, binding in justice on the other party to the contract, added to a matrimonial contract which is already complete and perfect. Since a mode, as a mode in the true sense, is thus added to an already existing and completed contract, it can have no effect on the validity of that contract. For example, two persons validly contract a marriage; then the husband adds a note which is contrary to the indissoluble substance of marriage, such as: "I marry you, but you must assume the obligation of helping me find a wife more worthy of my status." The mode, even though opposed to the substance of marriage, comes to the contract which is already complete and unencumbered. It cannot, therefore, have any effect on the validity of that contract, and it is to be disregarded as if it had not been added at all.

Still there was great disagreement among authors as to whether a mode, contrary to the substance of marriage, will or will not invalidate that contract of marriage. Sanchez and many who followed his opinion declared that a mode is to be considered as not added, unless it is opposed to the substance or an essential blessing of marriage, in which case it invalidates the contract, as does any contrary condition. An impossible or immoral mode, inasmuch as it thereby becomes indistinguishable from a resolvent condition, invalidates the contract. The reason is that in a mode of this kind, as also in the resolvent condition, the consent of the contracting party is made to depend on the fulfillment of the modification.[128]

---

[127] Cf. Sanchez, *op. cit.*, Lib. V, Disp. XIX, pp. 320-321; Soto, *Commentarium*, II, Dist. 29, Q. II, Art. I, p. 179; Pirhing, *Ius Canonicum*, Lib. IV, Tit. V, n. xxix, Ass. I, p. 69; Reiffenstuel, *Ius Canonicum Universum*, Lib. IV, Tit. V, n. 61, p. 438; Schmalzgrueber, *Ius Ecclesiasticum*, Lib. IV, Tit. V, § VI, n. 136, p. 444; Maschat, *Institutiones Canonicae*, Pars II, Lib. IV, Tit. V, n. 23, p. 351; Wernz, *Ius Decretalium*, IV, Tit. X, Schol. II, p. 452.

[128] Cf. Sanchez, *op. cit.*, Lib. V, Disp. XIX, n. 5, p. 321; Barbosa, *Collectanae*, Vol. II, Lib. IV, Tit. V, n. 5, p. 45; Gonzales-Tellez, *Commentaria*, Lib. IV, Tit. V, Cap. VII, p. 119; Pirhing, *Ius Canonicum*, Lib. IV, Tit. V, n. XXX, Assertio

The proponents of the opposite opinion distinguished between a condition which is part of the contract and directly affects it and a mode which accrues to a contract already complete in itself and merely adds to the contract a new agreement. For this reason these authors declared that such a modification, added to a completed contract, can have no effect on its validity, and it is therefore to be considered as an *impossible* condition, if a condition at all, and is to be regarded as *non adiecta*.[129]

When one considers the explanations of the authors, however, their disagreement on this point seems more apparent than real; it is a matter of terminology for the most part, depending rather on the manner in which the authors explain the concept of mode, than on the doctrine involved. If one considers the mode in the sense proposed by Reiffenstuel, Schmalzgrueber, etc., namely as accruing to a contract already complete, such an addition can have no effect on a contract already valid or invalid in itself. All the authors agree, however, that if any mode can be reduced to the status of a resolvent condition against the indissoluble nature of marriage, then it invalidates that contract. If it cannot be reduced to a condition contrary to the substance of marriage, but accrues as a mode to an already perfected and completed consent, then it has no effect on the validity. Each case will have to be examined in its variant circumstances before it can be determined whether there is a true condition against the substance in the intent of the parties to the contract, which condition is expressed as a mode, or just the addition of some further obligation to an unconditional and absolute consent.

---

2 and n. XXXI, Assertio 3, pp. 69-70; Schmier, *Iurisprudentia*, II, Lib. IV, Tract. II, Cap. II, Sec. III, § III nn. 143-147, p. 397; Pichler, *Ius Canonicum*, Lib. IV, Tit. V, n. 15, p. 542; De Angelis, *Praelectiones*, Lib. IV, Tit. V, n. 7, p. 155.

[129] Cf. Soto, *Commentarium*, II, Dist. 29, Q. II, Art. I, p. 179; Reiffenstuel, *Ius Canonicum Universum*, Lib. IV, Tit. V, #2, nn. 63-64, pp. 438-439; Leurenius, *Forum Ecclesiasticum, in Quo Ius Canonicum Universum . . . Explanatur* (5 vols., Venetiis, 1729), Lib. IV, Tit. V, Q. 177, pp. 70-71; Schmalzgrueber, *Ius Ecclesiasticum*, Lib. IV, Tit. V, § VI, n. 143, p. 447; Gasparri, *De Matrimonio*, II, Cap. IV, Art. IV, n. 978, p. 77; Maschat, *Institutiones Canonicae*, Pars II, Lib. IV, Tit. V, n. 23, p. 351; Grandclaude, *Ius Canonicum iuxta Ordinem Decretalium* (3 vols., Parisiis, 1882-1883), II, Lib. IV, Tit. V, Resp. 2, p. 87.

It can happen frequently that, as Wernz contented, theoretically a mode is simply added to a completed consent and cannot affect the validity, while, in practice, one could follow the opinion of Sanchez who maintained that a mode contrary to the substance of marriage, if added at the time of the contract, manifests the disposition of the mind of the contracting parties, so that the marriage is to be considered invalid for lact of consent.[130]

Naturally, this incidental indication of the contrary will of the parties cannot justify a *presumption* that will, in itself, overthrow the favor of law which marriage enjoys by canon 1014. The only presumption in law regarding marriage, with the exception noted for the privilege of the Faith in canon 1127, is for validity, not for invalidity.

D. Conclusion

The marital consent can be modified in different ways: by the addition of a condition from which the consent of the parties is to depend, or by the addition of a mode, a cause or a demonstration, or by the application of a time clause to the beginning or the termination of the contract. A condition which is contrary to the indissolubility of the contract invalidates the contract; modes, causes and demonstrations do not fundamentally or inherently (*per se*) invalidate the contract. It is always to be kept in mind, however, that the invalidating effect does not derive from the grammatical structure in which a modification is couched, but from the intention of the party or parties to the contract, as is evinced by the modification. Even if grammatically the external expression is in the form of a mode, or of a cause, or of a demonstration, the person may intend it as a condition *sine qua non,* and thus he or she does not give consent to the marriage except under this condition. Conversely, one may, in the seeming form of an invalidating condition, give

---

[130] "Si modus sit contrarius *substantiae* matrimonii, compluribus scriptoribus videtur irritare matrimonium. Cui sententia facile *in praxi* standum est . . . At *theoretice* verus modus pro natura sua oneris *adiecti* ad contractum *iam perfectum* non irritat contractum matrimonialem, etiamsi sit contra substantiam matrimonii." The reason as given by Wernz is: ". . . quoniam onus in forma modi contractui matrimoniali adiectum re et intentione contrahentium saepe potest esse nihil aliud quam *simulata conditio* in pactum deducta."—Wernz, *Ius Decretalium*, IV, Tit. X, Schol. II, p. 451.

expression to what is intended purely as a further obligation accruing to a contractual consent that in every respect is to be honored as valid.

Marriage is always to be presumed valid, but this presumption must yield to the truth whenever it can be proved that one of the parties entered the marriage with a condition contrary to the substance of marriage, intending not to contract marriage otherwise than under the invoked condition. In that event there is a defect of the consent requisite for the making of a valid marriage contract, and no power on earth can supply for that defect except the contracting parties.[131]

From the foregoing doctrine two deductions emerge. In the external forum of the Church any intention against the essential property of indissolubility in the matrimonial contract must be established by proof before the marriage contract can be branded as invalid. In the forum of conscience, however, the contract will be invalid if either or both of the parties thereto qualified consent for the marital union by way of any condition or intention which excludes the sacramental stability essential to marriage.

---

[131] Cf. Pirhing, *Ius Canonicum*, Lib. IV, Tit. V, n. XXXII, nota 2, p. 70.

CONCLUSIONS

Part I—Historical Synopsis

I. The doctrine of St. Augustine, while providing the theological basis for the doctrine on indissolubility and the terminology for future canonical development, did not treat the problem of conditions contrary to indissolubility. because the contractual aspect of marriage had not been thoroughly developed at his time. (Cf. p. 6).

II. Up to the thirteenth century authors were still at variance on many points regarding this doctrine, since they were still groping for the correct meaning of the term *"sacramentum"* in the expression *"bonum sacramenti."* (Cf. pp. 8-9).

III. Clear and definite legislation on the matter of conditions contrary to the indissolubility of the marriage bond came only during the pontificate of Gregory IX. (Cf. pp. 11-12).

IV. The *"Additiones"* to the *Summa Aurea Hostiensis,* which had been attributed to a certain Martinus, should correctly be attributed to Monaldus, a Franciscan canonist of the late thirteenth century. (Cf. pp. 15-16, footnote 16).

V. The Council of Trent enacted no new substantive law on conditions contrary to indissolubility, for no new law was needed; the nullifying law of Gregory's Decretal in this regard was to remain in force. (Cf. p. 19).

VI. By the beginning of the seventeenth century there was solidly established the essential doctrine on the invalidity of a marriage contract to which a condition contrary to indissolubility had been attached. (Cf. pp. 19-20).

Part II—Canonical Commentary

I. The objection of some modern authors to the application of the term "contract" to marriage in view of the specific differences between the marriage contract and other human contracts cannot be sustained; marriage is, in the truest sense, a contract, although it is of a unique character. (Cf. pp. 45-46).

II. Since the *bonum sacramenti* pertains in a special way to the essence of marriage, it occupies in its demand for the indissolubility of the union the preeminent rank among the three blessings of marriage. (Cf. p. 52).

III. For a valid matrimonial consent, an actual, a virtual or a habitual consent can suffice for the effecting of a valid marriage; the so-called interpretative consent can not suffice, since it represents a hypothesis, not a consent. (Cf. pp. 60-61).

IV. For proof of the presence of a condition or intention contrary to the stability of marriage, it is not required that the condition have been invoked or the intention conceived in the form of an express pact or agreement; such a condition or intention can juridically be recognized as present either upon an explicit declaration of one or both of the parties or in consequence of certain words or actions with a full, though only implicit, import to that effect, or, finally, as a result of the telling circumstances surrounding the contract, as long as these factors are duly established through juridically acceptable proof. (Cf. pp. 72-73; pp. 121-123).

V. Since a person who truly wills marriage must will it as it truly exists in nature, namely with all its essential elements, it follows that in the absence of a contrary intention, either actual or virtual, which excludes indissolubility from the contract, the general intention to marry, when expressed in the act of matrimonial consent, will effect a valid marriage, provided that the party is cognizant of the elements of the consent of marriage as delineated in canon 1082. (Cf. pp. 111-112).

VI. For this reason a simple error, that is, one which does not lead to the placing of a contrary condition or intention, will not invalidate the marriage contract, and, in consequence, by reason of the favor that marriage enjoys in law, every error will be presumed to be a simple error until there is proof that it qualified the consent of the will itself. (Cf. pp. 128-136).

VII. In the forum of conscience, however, any intention or condition contrary to the indissolubility of the bond, no matter in what way it may be expressed grammatically, invalidates the contract. This is so, regardless of the form the contrary intention takes, whether in connection with or apart from a pact, whether established by one or by both of the parties, whether internal or external, whether implicit or explicit, and whether in the form of a condition, of a mode, or of any other qualification of the consent. The reason for this is that any intention or condition which uproots the consent eradicates the marriage as well, since *"matrimonium facit partium consensus."* (Cf. pp. 126-127).

VIII.   The disagreement among the authors regarding the invalidating effect of a mode contrary to the substance of marriage represents a difference of terminology rather than a divergence of doctrine. (Cf. p. 147).

BIBLIOGRAPHY

Sources

Acta Apostolicae Sedis, Commentarium Officiale, Romae, 1909—

Acta Sanctae Sedis, In Compendium Opportune Redacta et Illustrata, studio et cura Josephi Pennacchi et Victorii Piazzesi, 41 vols., Romae: Typis Polyglottae Officinae S.C. de Propoganda Fide, 1865-1908.

Bible, The Holy, translated from the Latin Vulgate, Douay-Rheims version, New York: C. Wildermann Co. Inc., 1912.

Bullarium Ordinis Praedicatorum, ed. a T. Ripoll, recognitum a A. Bremond, 8 vols., Romae, 1729-1740.

Canones et Decreta Concilii Tridentini, edito Neapolitana Josephi Palella, Neopoli, 1859.

Codex Iuris Canonici, Pii X Pontificis Maximi iussu digestus, Benedicti Papae XV auctoritate promulgatus, Praefatione, Fontium Annotatione et Indice Analytico-Alphabetico, ab Emo Petro Card. Gasparri Auctus, Romae: Typis Polyglottis Vaticanis, 1917; reimpressio, 1934.

Codicis Iuris Canonici Fontes, cura Emi Petri Card. Gasparri editi, 9 vols., Romae (postea Civitate Vaticana): Typis Polyglottis Vaticanis, 1923-1939 (Vols. VII-IX, ed. cura et studio Emi Iustiniani Card. Secrédi).

Collectanea Sacrae Congregationis de Propoganda Fide, 2 vols., Romae: Typographia Polyglotta S. C. de Propoganda Fide, 1907.

Corpus Iuris Canonici, 2. ed. Lipsiensis, post Aemilii Ludovici Richteri curas instruxit Aemilius Friedberg, 2 vols., Lipsiae: Ex Officina Bernhardi Tauchnitz, 1879-1881; ed. anastatice repetita, Lipsiae: Tauchnitz, 1928.

Decretales D. Gregorii IX, una cum Glossis Restitutae, 2. vols., Romae, 1582.

Decretum Gratiani emendatum et notationibus illustratum, una cum glossis, Gregorii XIII Pont. Max. iussu editum, 3 vols., Taurini, 1588.

Denzinger, Heinrich—Bannwart, Clemens—Umberg, Joannes—Rahner, Carolus, *Enchiridion Symbolorum Definitionum et Declarationum de Rebus et Morum*, 28. ed., augmentata, Friburgi Brisgoviae: Herder, 1952.

Patrologiae Cursus Completus, Series Latina, ed. Jacques Paul Migne, 221 vols., Parisiis, 1844-1864.

Potthast, A., *Regesta Pontificum Romanorum*, inde ab anno post Christum natum MCXVIII ad annum MCCCIV, 2 vols., Berolini, 1874-1875.

Sacrae Romanae Rotae Decisiones seu Sententiae, quae iuxta Legem Propriam et Constitutionem "Sapienti Consilio" Pii PP. X prodierunt, cura eiusdem S. Tribunalis editae, 38 vols., Romae, 1912—

Testament, The New—A Revision of the Challoner-Rheims Version, Confraternity Edition, Paterson, N. J.: St. Anthony Guild Press, 1941.

Thesaurus Resolutionum Sacrae Congregationis Concilii, 167 vols., Urbino: vols. I-V, 1739-1740; Romae: vols. VI ff., 1741-1908.

154 *Bibliography*

REFERENCE WORKS

Amort, Eusebius, *Elementa Iuris Canonici Veteris et Moderni*, Vol. II, *Ius Canonicum Modernum*, Ferrariae, 1763.

Anselm of Lucca, *Anselmi Lucensis Collectio Canonum*, ed. a F. Thaner, Innsbruck, 1906-1915.

Augustinus, Antonius, *Quinque Compilationes Antiquae*, Ilerdae, 1576.

Ayrinhac, H. A.-Lydon, P., *Marriage Legislation in the New Code of Canon Law*, revised ed., New York: Benziger Brothers, 1949.

Bangen, Joannes H., *Instructio Practica de Sponsalibus et Matrimonio in Usum Sacerdotum Curatorum*, Monasterii, typis et sumptibus librariae Aschendorffianae, 1858-1860.

Barbosa, Augustinus, *Collectanea Doctorum tam Veterum quam Recentiorum in Ius Pontificium Universum*, 3 vols., Romae, 1626.

Bayon, J.-Garcia, F., *Tractatus Canonico-Moralis de Sacramento Matrimonii*, 2 vols. in 1, Madrid, 1931

Benedictus XIV (Prosper Lambertini), *De Synodo Dioecesana*, 4 vols., Romae, 1783.

Bender, L., cf. Vlaming, T.

Beste, Udalricus, *Introductio in Codicem*, 3 ed., Collegeville, Minn.: St. John's Abbey Press, 1946.

Bonfanti, *Instituzioni di Diritto Romano*, Romae, 1934.

Bouscaren, T. Lincoln, *The Canon Law Digest*, 3 vols., Milwauwee: Bruce, 1934—1954. *Supplements*, 1953 through 1955 (James O'Connor, co-editor).

Bouscaren, T. L.-Ellis, A. C., *Canon Law, a Text and Commentary*, 2. ed., 2nd printing, Milwaukee: Bruce, 1953.

Cappello, Felix M., *Summa Iuris Canonici*, 3 vols., Vol. II, 4. ed., Romae, apud Aedes Universitatis Gregorianae, 1945.

———, *Tractatus Canonico-Moralis de Sacramentis*, editio quarta emendata et aucta, 3 vols. in 4, Augustae Taurinorum: Marietti, 1944.

Chelodi, Ioannes, *Ius Canonicum de Matrimonio et de Iudiciis Matrimonialibus*, 5. ed., recognita et aucta a Pio Ciprotti, Vicenza: Societa Anonima Tipografica Editrice, 1947.

Coronata, Matthaeus Conte a, *Institutiones Iuris Canonici, De Sacramentis Tractatus Canonicus*, Vol. III, De Matrimonio et de Sacramentalibus, Romae: Marietti, 1943: ed. altera et emendata, Romae: Marietti, 1947.

Corpus Scriptorum Ecclesiasticorum Latinorum, 71 vols., Pragae, Vindobonae, Lipsiae, 1866—

Courtemanche, Basil F., *The Total Simulation of Matrimonial Consent*, The Catholic University of America Canon Law Studies, n. 270, Washington, D.C.: The Catholic University of America Press, 1948.

Covarruvias y Leyva, *Omnia Opera*, 2 vols., Coloniae Allobrogum, 1679.

De Angelis, Phillipus, *Praelectiones Iuris Canonici,* 5 vols., Romae-Parisiis, 1877-1891.

De Becker, Julius, *De Sponsalibus et Matrimonio Praelectiones Canonicae,* ed. nova, Louvain: Fr. Ceuterick, 1931.

De Lugo, Joannes, *Omnia Opera, Disputationes de Iustitia et Iure,* Vol. II, Venetiis, 1718.

———, *Disputationes de Sacramentis in Genere,* Vol. V, Venetiis, 1718.

De Smet, Aloysius, *Tractatus Theologico-Canonicus de Sponsalibus et Matrimonio,* ed. 4., Brugis: Car. Bayaert, 1927.

Devoti, Joannes, *Institutiones Canonicae,* 4. ed., 4 vols., Venetiis, 1827.

Doheny, William J., *Canonical Procedure in Matrimonial Cases,* Vol. I, *Formal Judicial Procedure,* 2. ed., Milwaukee: Bruce, 1948.

Durandus, Gulielmus, *Speculum Judiciale,* Venetiis, 1577.

Esmein, A., par Genestal, R. et Dauvillier, J., *Le Mariage en Droit Canonique,* 2 vols., Parisiis: Recueil-Siray, 1929-1935.

Fagnanus, Prosper, *Commentaria in V Libros Decretalium,* Venetiis, 1709.

Fournier, Paul, *Les Collections Canoniques Attribuées à Yves de Chartres,* Parisiis, 1897.

Fraghi, D., *De Conditionibus Matrimonio Appositis,* Romae: Officium Libri Catholici, 1941.

Gasparri, Petrus Card., *Tractatus Canonicus de Matrimonio,* editio nova ad mentem Codicis I. C., 2 vols., Typis Polyglottis Vaticanis, 1932 (post-Code); 3. ed., Parisiis, 1904.

Gerdilius, Giacinto Segismondo Card., *Trattato del Matrimonio,* Romae, 1803.

Gonzales-Tellez, Emmanuel, *Commentaria Perpetua in Singulos Textus V Librorum Decretalium Gregorii IX,* Vol. IV, Lugduni, 1673.

Grandclaude, E., *Ius Canonicum iuxta Ordinem Decretalium,* 3 vols., Parisiis, 1882-1883.

Griese, N. Orville, *The Marriage Contract and the Procreation of Offspring,* The Catholic University of America Canon Law Studies, n. 226, Washington, D.C.: The Catholic University of America Press, 1946.

Guido a Baiiso, *Rosarium seu in Decretorum Volumen Commentaria,* Venetiis, 1577.

Gutierrez, Joannes, *Iurisconsulti Praeclarissimi Hispani Canonicarum Quaestionum Utriusque Fori,* Nurembergae, 1647.

Hostiensis, Card. Henricus de Segusio, *Commentaria in Quinque Decretalium Libros,* 5 vols. in 3, Venetiis, 1581.

———, *Summa Aurea, Venetiis,* 1570.

Innocentius IV, *Commentaria in V Libros Decretalium,* Vol. IV, Venetiis, 1570.

Ioannes Andreae, *Commentarium in Sextum Decretalium de Regulis Iuris,* Venetiis, 1581.

Joyce, H., *Christian Marriage,* 2. ed., London: Sheed and Ward, 1948.

LaCroix, Claudius, *Theologiae Moralis,* Vol. VI, *De Sacramentis,* Coloniae, 1719.

Lambertini, Prosper, cf. Benedict XIV.

Lancellotus, Ioannes Paulus, *Institutiones Iuris Canonici,* Venetiis, 1704.

Laymann, Paulus, *Theologia Moralis*, Venetiis, 1630.

Leurenius, Petrus, *Forum Ecclesiasticum, in Quo Ius Canonicum Universum ... Explanatur*, 5 vols., Venetiis, 1729.

Mackay, Richard V., *Laws of Marriage and Divorce Simplified*, 2. ed., by Irving Mandell, Legal Almanac Series, New York: Oceana Publications, 1954.

Martin of Azpilcueta, cf. Navarrus.

Maschat, Remigius, *Institutiones Canonicae*, Romae, 1757.

Navarrus, *Enchiridion sive Manuale Confessariorum et Penitentium*, Venetiis, 1593.

————, *Omnia Opera in VI Tomos Distributa*, Venetiis, 1618.

Noldin, H.-Schmitt, A., *Summa Theologiae Moralis iuxta Codicem Iuris Canonici*, 3 vols., 27. ed., Ratisbonae-Romae-Neo-Eboraci: Pustet, 1940.

Panormitanus, (Nicholaus de Tudeschis), *Commentaria in Quinque Libros Decretalium*, 5 vols. in 7, Venetiis, 1588.

Paucapalea, *Summa Paucapaleae, Die Summa des Paucapalea über das Decretum Gratiani*, ed. a J. F. von Schulte, Giessen, 1890.

Payen, G., *De Matrimonio in Missionibus ac Potissimum in Sinis Tractatus Practicus et Casus*, 2. ed., 3 vols., Zi-ka-wei, 1935-1936.

Perrone, Ioannes, *De Matrimonio Christiano*, 3 vols., Romae, 1858.

Pichler, Vitus, *Ius Canonicum secundum V Decretalium Titulos Explicatum*, 2 vols., Ravennae, 1741.

Pirhing, Ernricus, *Ius Canonicum in V Libros Decretalium nova Methodo Explicatum*, ed. novissima, 4 vols., Dilingae, 1722.

Pontius, Basilius, *Tractatus de Sacramento Matrimonii; Appendix De Matrimonio Catholici cum Heretico*, Venetiis, 1756.

Raymond of Pennafort, *Summa Sancti Raymundi*, Veronae, 1744.

Reiffenstuel, Anacletus, *Ius Canonicum Universum*, 5 vols. in 7, Parisiis, 1864-1882.

Reuter, Amandus, *S. Aurelii Augustini Doctrina de Bonis Matrimonii*, Analecta Gregoriana, Vol. XXVII (Series Theologica, Sectio B, n. 12), Romae: Apud Aedes Universitatis Gregorianae, 1942.

Rimlinger, Herbert T., *Error Invalidating Matrimonial Consent*, The Catholic University of America Canon Law Studies, n. 82, Washington, D.C.: The Catholic University of America, 1932.

Rolandus Bandinelli, *Die Summa Magistri Rolandi Bandinelli nachmals Papstes Alexander III.*, ed. F. Thaner, Innsbruck, 1874.

Rufinus, *Die Summa Decretorum des Magister Rufinus*, ed. Heinrich Singer, Paderborn, 1902.

Sanchez, Thomas, *De Sancto Matrimonii Sacramento Disputationum Tomi Tres*, 10 libri in 3 vols., Venetiis, 1726.

Schmalzgrueber, Franciscus, *Ius Ecclesiasticum Universum*, 5 vols. in 12, Romae, 1843-1845.

Schmier, Franciscus, *Iurisprudentia Canonico-Civilis, seu Ius Canonicum Universum*, 2 vols., Venetiis, 1754.

Schulte, Johann Friedrich von, *Die Geschichte der Quellen und Literatur des canonischen Rechts,* von Papst Gregor IX. bis zum Concil von Trient, Stuttgart: Enke, 1877.

————, cf. also Paucapalea; Stephanus Tornacensis.

Singer, cf. **Rufinus.**

Sipos, Stephanus, *Enchiridion Iuris Canonici,* 6. ed. a L. Gálas, Romae: Herder, 1954.

Smith, Vincent M., *Ignorance Affecting Matrimonial Consent,* The Catholic University of America Canon Law Studies, n. 245, Washington, D.C.: The Catholic University of America Press, 1950.

Soto, Dominicus, *Commentarium in Quartum Librum Sententiarum,* Vol. II, Venetiis, 1584.

Staffa, Dinus, *De Conditione Contra Matrimonii Substantiam,* Romae: Apud Custodiam Librariam Pont. Instituti Utriusque Iuris, 1952.

Stephanus Tornacensis, *Die Summa des Stephanus Tornacensis über das Decretum Gratiani,* ed. Johann Friedrich von Schulte, Giessen, 1891.

Sylvester Prierias, *Summa Sylvestrina,* Venetiis, 1601.

Tellez, cf. Gonzales-Tellez.

Thaner, F., cf. Rolandus.

Thomas, John L., *The American Catholic Family,* Englewood Cliffs, N. J.: Prentice-Hall, Inc., 1956.

Timlin, Bartholomew, *Conditional Matrimonial Consent,* The Catholic University of America Canon Law Studies, n. 89, Washington, D.C.: The Catholic University of America, 1934.

Van Espen, Zeger, *Ius Ecclesiasticum Universum,* Lovanii, 1732.

Van Hove, Alphonsus, *Commentarium Lovaniense in Codicem Iuris Canonici,* 1 vol. in 5 tomes, Tomus I, *Prolegomena,* 2. ed., Mechliniae-Romae: Dessain, 1945.

Vermeersch, A.-Creusen, J., *Epitome Iuris Canonici,* 3. ed., 3 vols., Mechliniae-Romae: H. Dessain, 1927-1928.

Vlaming, Thomas M., *Praelectiones Iuris Matrimonii,* 4. ed., a L. Bender, O.P., Bussum in Hollandia: Paulus Brand, 1950.

Vromant, G., *Ius Missionariorum,* 6 vols., Vol. V, *De Matrimonio,* Lovanii: Museum Lessianum, 1931.

Wanenmacher, Franciscus, *The Evidence in Ecclesiastical Procedure Affecting the Marriage Bond,* The Catholic University of America Canon Law Studies, n. 9 (1920); printed in Philadelphia, Pa.: The Dolphin Press, 1935.

Wernz, Franciscus, *Ius Decretalium ad Usum Praelectionum in Scholis Textus Canonici sive Iuris Decretalium,* 6 vols. in 10, Romae et Prati, 1898-1914.

Wernz, F.-Vidal, P., *Ius Canonicum,* Vol. V., *Ius Matrimoniale,* 3. ed. a P. Aguirre, Romae: Apud Aedes Universitatis Gregorianae, 1946.

ARTICLES

Burke, Edward M., "Perpetuity in the Marriage Bond," *The Jurist,* XIV (1954), 47-59.

Kuttner, Stephen, "Bernardus Compostellanus Antiquus," *Traditio: Studies in Ancient and Medieval History, Thought and Religion*, I (1943), 283-284.
Pellegrini, B., "De Intentione Bono Sacramenti Adversa Eiusdemque Probatione in Iudicio ad Normam Can. 1086," *Ius Pontificium*, IX (1929), 306-311.
Quinn, Andrew, "Defects in Marriage Consent," *The Jurist*, V (1945), 532-551.

PERIODICALS

Apollinaris, Romae, 1928—
Jurist, The, Washington, D.C., 1941—
Jus Pontificium, Romae, 1921-1940.
Traditio, New York, 1943—

ABBREVIATIONS

AAS	—*Acta Apostolicae Sedis*
ASS	—*Acta Sanctae Sedis*
Collectanea	—*Collectanea S. Congregationis de Propoganda Fide*
CSEL	—*Corpus Scriptorum Ecclesiasticorum Latinorum*
Decisiones	—*Sacrae Romanae Rotae Decisiones seu Sententiae*
Fontes	—*Codicis Iuris Canonici Fontes*, cura—Gasparri editi
MPL	—Migne, *Patrologiae Cursus Completus, Series Latina*
Potthast	—*Regesta Pontificum Romanorum*
S.C.C.	—*Sacra Congregatio Concilii*
S.C. de Prop. Fide	— *Sacra Congregatio de Propoganda Fide*
S.C.S. Off.	—*Sacra Congregatio Sancti Officii*
S.R. Rota	—*Sacra Romana Rota*
Thesaurus	—*Thesaurus Resolutionum Sacrae Congregationis Concilii*

INDEX OF AUTHORS

ALPHABETICAL INDEX

BIOGRAPHICAL NOTE

Dennis J. Burns was born in Cambridge, Massachusetts, on November 21, 1920. He received his elementary education in that city at Blessed Sacrament and Saint Peter's Parochial Schools, under the direction of the Sisters of Notre Dame de Namur and the School Sisters of Notre Dame respectively. In June, 1938, he graduated from Saint Francis Xavier High School in Duxbury, Massachusetts, and in September of that year entered Sacred Heart College in Girard, Pennsylvania, both of which were conducted by the Fathers of the Divine Word.

In June of 1940, after two years of college, he entered Saint Mary's Seminary in Techny, Illinois, where he finished his studies in philosophy and completed the requirements for the degree of Bachelor of Arts in 1944. Having completed two years of theological studies in Saint Mary's, he entered Saint John's Seminary in Brighton, Massachusetts, in September, 1946, and there continued his training in theology.

He was ordained to the sacred priesthood at the Cathedral of the Holy Cross, Boston, Massachusetts, on May 3, 1950, by the Most Reverend Richard J. Cushing, D.D., Archbishop of Boston, for the service of that archdiocese. He served as assistant priest at Saint Jude's Parish, Waltham, for three and a half years, and at Saint John's - Saint Hugh's Parish, Roxbury, for another year.

In October, 1954, he was assigned to pursue further studies in the School of Canon Law of the Catholic University of America, from which he received the degree of the Baccalaureate in Canon Law in June, 1955, and the degree of the Licentiate in Canon Law in June, 1956.

CANON LAW STUDIES*

375. Kelleher, Rev. Francis T., A.B., J.C.L., Judicial expenses.
376. Bantigue, Rev. Pedro N., J.C.L., The Provincial Council of Manila of 1771. (Its text followed by a commentary on *Actio II, De Episcopis*)
377. Burns, Rev. Dennis J., A.B., J.C.L., Matrimonial indissolubility: contrary conditions.
378. Deutsch, Rev. Bernard F., J.C.L., Jurisdiction of pastors in the external forum.
379. Dunnivan, Rev. John P., A.B., J.C.L., Prejudicial attempts in pending litigation.
380. Ernst, Rev. Albert C., A.B., J.C.L., Free admission to Church for sacred rites.
381. Frattin, Mr. Peter Louis, J.C.L., The matrimonial impediment of impotence: occlusion of the spermatic ducts and vaginismus.
382. Henry, Rev. Charles W., O.S.B., A.B., S.T.L., J.C.L., Canonical relations between bishops and abbots at the beginning of the tenth century.
383. Hoffman, Rev. Lawrence J., A.B., J.C.L., Clergy conference: Canon 131.
384. Markham, Rev. James, A.B., S.T.L, J.C.L., The Sacred Congregation of Seminaries and Universities of Studies.
385. McGrath, Rev. John J., A.B., LL.B., J.C.L., A comparative study of crime and its imputability in ecclesiastical criminal law and in American criminal law.
386. McGuire, Rev. James D., O.R.S.A., J.C.L., The postulancy.
387. Munday, Rev. James E., J.C.L., Ecclesiastical Property in Australia and New Zealand.
388. Murphy, Rev. Joseph P., A.B., J.C.L., The laws of the State of New York affecting church property.
389. Pickard, Rev. William M., J.C.L., Judicial experts: a source of evidence in ecclesiastical trials.
390. Ruddy, Rev. James, J.C.L., The Apostolic Constitution *Christus Dominus*: text, translation and commentary, with short annotations on the Motu Proprio *Sacram Communionem*.
391. Vanyo, Rev. Leo V., A.B., J.C.L., Requisites of intention in the reception of the sacraments.

---

* For a complete list of the available numbers of this series apply to the Catholic University of America Press, 620 Michigan Avenue, N.E., Washington (17), D.C., for a general catalogue.

CPSIA information can be obtained
at www.ICGtesting.com
Printed in the USA
BVHW032131180119
538228BV00005B/137/P